AF600539

PROFESSION OF FAITH

THE CATHOLIC UNIVERSITY OF AMERICA
CANON LAW STUDIES
No. 151

PROFESSION OF FAITH

BY

WALTER JOSEPH CANAVAN, Litt.D., J.C.L.
Priest of the Archdiocese of Denver

A DISSERTATION

Submitted to the Faculty of the School of Canon Law of the Catholic University of America in Partial Fulfillment of the Requirements for the Degree of

DOCTOR OF CANON LAW

CATHOLIC UNIVERSITY OF AMERICA PRESS
WASHINGTON, D. C.
1942

NIHIL OBSTAT

EDWARDUS ROELKER, J.C.D.,

Censor Deputatus.

Washingtonii, D. C., die XXV Maii, 1942.

IMPRIMATUR

URBANUS IOANNES VEHR, D.D.,

Archiepiscopus Denveriensis.

Denveri, Colo., die XV, Augusti, 1942.

PRINTED IN THE UNITED STATES OF AMERICA
BY THE REGISTER COLLEGE OF JOURNALISM,
DENVER, COLO.

TO
MY PARENTS
AND
FRIENDS

TABLE OF CONTENTS

PART TWO—CANONICAL COMMENTARY

CHAPTER IV

CHAPTER V

CHAPTER VI

CHAPTER VII

CHAPTER VIII

CHAPTER IX

FOREWORD

The Church is ever vigilant about the faith that has been committed to her care by the Divine Master. In every age, therefore, she has been careful lest the truths of which she is the champion be lost through carelessness or destroyed by heresy. She has since her founding demanded that her ministers be conspicuous in their profession of that faith, that her children manifest it frequently during life, that her erring sons and daughters pronounce their adherence to the chief truths of that faith when they return to the fold. It is the purpose of the present work to outline those institutions of Papal, conciliar, and synodal origin that finally developed into the legislation on the profession of faith, which legislation is now contained in the Code of Canon Law in canons 1406-1408.

In the historical portion of this thesis an attempt is made to trace the canonical processes of the profession of faith from the early days of the Church to the time of the promulgation of the Code. It is not the purpose of the work, however, to consider specifically the history of the profession of faith that is required for Baptism. Nor does the thesis consider at length that profession of faith required of heretics who enter the Church. Only when an example of these professions explains the progress of the canonical rather than the liturgical institute of the profession of faith is it considered. The treatment of the historical progress of the subject is chronological rather than topical. The thesis proposes to show the final crystallization of the institute of the profession of faith into the legislation of the Council of Trent and the pronouncements of Pope Pius IV, which form the basis of the present law.

Most of the canonical commentators do not consider canons 1406-1408 in detail. Several problems need to be discussed, however, as, for example, the infliction of penalties for the violation of these canons. It is the purpose of the canonical portion of this work to state these problems and to solve them in the measure in which that can feasibly be done.

After a consideration of the formula of profession, the obligation of those mentioned in canon 1406, § 1, to make a profession of faith is discussed. Attention is given to the anti-Modernist oath, which is closely allied to the subject matter, and to the informal profession of faith demanded under certain circumstances by canon 1325, § 1. The penalties inflicted by law on those who fail to obey the precept of law regarding the profession of faith are also treated.

A sincere expression of gratitude is extended to the Most Rev. Urban J. Vehr, Archbishop of Denver, for the opportunity of graduate study in canon law; to the Rt. Rev. Monsignor Matthew J. W. Smith, Editor-in-chief of the *Register System of Newspapers*, for his many kindnesses; to the members of the Faculty of the School of Canon Law of the Catholic University of America for their helpful criticisms and suggestions, and to all who have in any way made this work possible.

PART I
HISTORICAL SYNOPSIS

CHAPTER I

ORIGINS OF PROFESSION OF FAITH

Article I. Nature of Profession of Faith

In every society there must be some external mark whereby its members are to be recognized. Since membership is to a great extent gauged by the external participation of the persons who make up an organization in the practices of that organization and by their external adherence to its tenets or principles, there must exist the means by which this manifestation of membership can be ascertained. It is only logical to assume, therefore, that the Church, the perfect society, has a specific means of identifying her members other than their internal belief and their participation in her sacraments and rites. Certainly this means is the outward confession of the members of the Church that they believe her doctrines. This outward confession of an internal belief is called the profession of faith.

Profession of faith is one of the signs or testaments by which true Christians are distinguished from heretics, schismatics, or infidels. It is usually an attestation that the one making it assents to the teachings of the Church; that he accepts what she accepts; that he rejects what she denies. This assent to the doctrines of the Church is expressed by the subscribing to some doctrinal formula or symbol that contains the principal dogmas of the church.[1]

It is probable that some doctrinal formula, however concise, was in use from the beginning of Christianity to secure uniformity in both teaching and belief and to place beyond doubt the orthodoxy of those who were admitted to the Church. It has been suggested that the knowledge and recitation of the symbol allegedly composed by the Apostles was a sort of password by which the Christians were able to know each other, especially in the days of the Roman persecutions, and whereby the followers of Christ who went into strange cities might

[1] "Credere autem non potest aliquis nisi ei veritas quam credat proponitur. Et ideo necessarium fuit fidei veritatem in unum collegi ut facilius posset omnibus proponi, ne aliquis per ignorantiam fidei a veritate dificeret. Et ab huiusmodi sententiarum fidei collectione nomen symboli est acceptum."—St. Thomas Aquinas, *Summa Theologica,* IIa IIae, q. 1, art. 9; cf. Wernz, *Ius Decretalium* (6 vols., Romae et Prati, 1898-1908; III, *Ius Administrationis Ecclesiae Catholicae,* Romae, 1908), III, n. 8.

recognize their fellows and secure the knowledge of the place where the Christians met and offered sacrifice.[2]

Although the New Testament is silent on the necessity of making a formal profession of faith, there is ample evidence that in the Scriptures a confession of faith is considered necessary. Early in His public life Our Divine Lord declared: "Therefore, everyone who acknowledges me before men, I will also acknowledge him before my Father in heaven."[3]

St. Paul in several of his Epistles is emphatic about the necessity of faith and its profession.[4]

The first public profession of faith on record in the Christian era is that of the Apostle Peter, who declared when Christ asked His disciples to tell Him of their belief as to His identity: "Thou art Christ, the Son of the living God." [5]

One of the first converts of the infant Church, the "eunuch of great authority" under Candace, Queen of the Ethopians, also made profession of faith in the Divinity of Christ when he desired Baptism at the hands of the Deacon Philip.[6]

The general public use of creeds or symbols began in connection with the reception of the Sacrament of Baptism, as a preparation for that rite and in response to the preliminary interrogations as to the fitness of the candidate for its reception. In the course of time the format of these creeds changed, not because the Church began to teach new truths, but because the errors of the heretics who arose from time to time needed to be discovered and refuted. In explaining this, St. Thomas wrote:

> . . . in omnibus symbolis eadem fidei docetur veritas; sed ibi oportet populum diligentius instrui de fidei veritate ubi errores insurgunt ne fides simplicium per haereticos corrumpatur.[7]

[2] Cf. Wernz, *loc. cit.;* Christianus Lupus, *Synodorum Generalium ac Provincialium Decreta et Canones* (9 vols., Venetiis, 1724-1727), I, 177.

[3] Matt., X, 32; Luke, XII, 8, 9; IX, 26. All Scriptural quotations used in this work are from *The New Testament,* Confraternity of Christian Doctrine revision (Paterson, N. J.: St. Anthony Guild Press, 1941).

[4] Cf. Rom., X, 10; Heb., X, 38; Gal., III, 11; Rom., I, 17.

[5] Matt., XVI, 16.

[6] Acts, VIII, 37.

[7] *Summa Theologica,* IIa IIae, q. 1, art. 9.

Article II. Evidences From the Fathers and Early Councils

There is no doubt that the first legislation on the profession of faith was liturgical and concerned the Sacrament of Baptism. As early as the time of the Deacon Philip a confession of belief in the Divinity of Christ was made before the reception of that sacrament. The great bulk of Christian converts for almost two centuries after Christ was composed of adults, and it was a custom which had the force of law that these make a profession of faith before they were received into the Church.[8]

The early Western Fathers bear witness to this liturgical practice in their writings. Tertullian speaks of the three attestations or professions of faith that were made by the one who received this sacrament.[9]

St. Augustine (354-430) in his *Confessions* gives interesting testimony of the practice of the profession of faith.[10]

The Western Fathers are, moreover, unanimous in testifying to the existence and use of a creed that was handed down by the Apostles and their successors. In a so-called letter of Pope St. Clement of Rome[11] to James, brother of the Lord, is to be found the following:

> Christo resurgente et ascendente in coelum, misso Sancto Spiritu, collata Apostolis scientia linguarum, adhuc in uno positi, *symbolum quod nunc fidelis tenet Ecclesia* unusquisque, quod sensit, dicendo, condiderunt; ut discedentes ab invicem hanc regulam per omnes praedicarent.[12]

[8] Cf. Wernz, *Ius Decretalium,* III, n. 13; Benedict XIV, *De Synodo Dioecesana* (2 vols., Romae, 1806), lib. V, cap. II, n. 9; Hinschius, *Das Kirchenrecht der Katholiken und Protestanten in Deutschland* (6 vols., Berlin, 1869-1897), III, 218.

[9] *De Baptismo,* C. 6.—Migne, *Patrologiae Cursus Completus, Series Latina* (221 vols., Parisiis, 1844-1864), I, 1206. Future references to this work will be indicated by the letters *MPL.*

[10] "Denique, ut ventum est ad horam profitendae fidei, quae verbis certis conceptis, retentisque memoriter, de loco eminentiore in conspectu populi fidelis Romae reddi solet ab eis qui accessuri sunt ad gratiam tuam, oblatum esse dicebat Victorino a presbyteris ut secretus redderet . . . illum autem maluisse salutem suam in conspectu sanctae multitudinis profiteri."—Lib. 8, c. 2—*MPL,* XXXII, 751, n. 5.

[11] It is unlikely that this letter is authentic. Very probably it was found in some early collection of decretals by the author of *Pseudo-Isidore* and given a talse inscription by him. Cf. Hinschius, *Decretales Pseudo-Isidorianae et Capitula Angilramni* (Lipsiae, 1863), p. 37.

[12] From the collection of the decretals of the Popes to be found in *Pseudo-Isidore—MPL,* CXXX, 27 D; cf. Hinschius, *loc. cit.*

Tertullian also speaks of a rule of faith that the Church received from the Apostles, the Apostles from Christ.[13]

St. Ambrose (340-379) in his *Explanatio Symboli ad Initiandos* declares that the Apostles collected the truths of faith into one short form in order that the faithful might quickly learn the whole series of truths of the Christian religion.[14]

St. Irenaeus (130-202) affirms in *Adversus Haereses* that the whole world professed the faith of the Apostles and their disciples.[15]

St. Jerome (340-420) bears witness that Origen sent to Pope Fabian (236-250) a profession of faith to explain his stand and to retract his errors.[16]

St. Cyprian (249-258) complains that the Novatian heretics had no scruples about subscribing to the symbol of faith, although they in truth denied what they professed.[17]

All of these opinions of the Western Fathers, while not showing the necessity of a set formula for the liturgical profession of faith in all instances, yet bear witness to the fact that at a very early period some sort of confessions of faith was deemed necessary.

The Eastern Fathers are no less definite in their testimony as to the practice of some kind of liturgical confession of faith in the Oriental Church. St. Cyril of Jerusalem (315-386) in his work, entitled *Catechesis III De Baptismo,* speaks of a profession of faith that had to be made by candidates before Baptism.[18]

St. John Chrysostom declares that it was a custom innaugurated by the Apostles that the symbol be recited by those who were about to receive Baptism.[19]

[13] *De S. Zeonis Operibus, Actis, Cultu et Aetate,* ad § III—*MPL,* II, 50; cf. also the other pronouncements of the same writer in *MPL,* II, 899, and *MPL,* II, 26.

[14] *MPL,* XVII, 1155.

[15] Lib. 1, C. 2—Migne, *Theologiae Cursus Completus* (28 vols., Parisiis, 1858-1864), VI, 386.

[16] *MPL,* XXI, 600.

[17] Epistle 76, *Ad Magnum—MPL,* III, 1146.

[18] Caput X—Migne, *Patrologiae Cursus Completus, Series Graeca* (161 vols., Parisiis, 1857-1866), XXXIII, 442, n. 7. Future references to this work will be made by the use of the letters *MPG.*

[19] Hom. LX ad I Corinthios—*MPG,* LXI, 343.

Christianus Lupus, commenting on the Nicene Creed, says the recitation of the Apostles' Creed was the foundation of the three rules of the early Christians—"*communicatio pacis, appellatio fraternitatis, et contesseratio hospitalitatis.*" He affirms that the password of hospitality among early Christians was the symbol. With it the follower of Christ could go through the world without money; the recitation of it would at once classify him as a Christian and assure him welcome by members of the Church wherever he might go.[20]

The history of the Church is filled with ever-recurring movements that opposed the Christian teaching in one point or another. These movements, called heresies, which arose as early as the late first century, necessarily led to legislation that would be an aid in the preservation of orthodoxy. It is not strange, therefore, that several of the very early synods held by the Church in various parts of the world regulated the manner of receiving those who had lapsed into heresy back into the Church. Invariably a profession of faith was demanded. The legislation enacted by these synods had only as much weight as the authority of the council or synod that enacted it. Thus, laws passed by an ecumenical council were universal in their application; those adopted by a particular council bound only the churches and persons in the ecclesiastical district of the council. First the pertinent enactments of general councils will be considered, and then attention will be directed to the legislation of the particular synods.

The Ecumenical Council of Nicaea (325) declared that the Novatianist clergy who returned to the Catholic Church might remain in the clerical state after they had certified in writing that they would accept and follow the teachings of the Church and after they had received the imposition of hands.[21] This legislation was specifically for the priests of the Novatian sect and cannot be considered as binding also priests of other heretical sects who came into the Church.[22] The same council also decreed that if a priest was admitted to the priesthood without examination, or if, upon inquiry, he confessed to a crime he had committed and had, nevertheless, received the imposition of hands, he was to be deposed.[23] Although there is no intrinsic

[20] *Op. cit.*, 182-183.

[21] Canon 8—Mansi, *Sacrorum Conciliorum Nova et Amplissima Collectio* (53 vols. in 59, Parisiis, 1901-1907), II, 680; cf. Hefele—Clark, *History of the Christian Councils* (5 vols., Edinburgh, 1883-1896), I, 410. Both of these works will henceforth be cited by the use of the authors' names.

[22] Hefele-Clark, I, 411.

[23] Canon 9—Mansi, II, 680; Hefele-Clark, I, 414; "The transgressions here referred to are all such as exclude a person from the priesthood, namely, idolatry,

evidence that the examination demanded by this canon of Nicaea included an inquiry into the faith of the candidate for the priesthood, which could be expressed by a profession of faith to the examiners, such a profession might well have been included in the examination. The Church was ever sedulous in choosing candidates for its priesthood [24] and certainly it would be sure of the faith of those about to be ordained. Such certainty could come only from the profession of the candidate that he believed in all the truths proposed by the Church. The II Ecumenical Council of the Church, held in Constantinople, established a precedent that is followed to this day and is embodied in the legislation of the Code of Canon Law,[25] for it professed the faith of the Council of Nicaea.[26] It also decreed that those entering the Church must anathematize in writing every heresy.[27] At the first session of the Ecumenical Council of Ephesus (431), those present began the proceedings by reading the Nicene Creed. They next affirmed that a letter of the Patriarch Cyril of Alexandria to Nestorius agreed with the Nicene faith.[28] At its sixth session the same council gave order, under pain of excommunication and deposition, that no other Creed than that of Nicaea should be professed.[29]

At the second session of the Ecumenical Council of Chalcedon (451), older documents in which Christian truth had already been set forth were publicly read. Among these documents were the following: (1) The faith of Nicaea; (2) the Creed of the Council of Constantinople; (3) the letter from the Patriarch Cyril to Nestorius and his letter to John, Patriarch of Antioch; (4) the famous *Epistola Dogmatica* of Pope Leo I. After these were read, the Fathers, according to Hefele-Clark, exclaimed: "This is the faith of the Fathers;

adultery, homicide, blasphemy, bigamy, heresy, etc. . . . The council draws attention first to the case of those who have been or in the future may be elevated to the priesthood without that examination required by I Tim., 3:2, and Tit., 1:7."—Schroeder, *Disciplinary Decrees of the General Councils* (St. Louis: B. Herder Book Co., 1937), p. 37.

[24] Cf. Schroeder, *loc. cit.*

[25] Canon 1406, § 1, 1°.

[26] Canon 1—Mansi, II, 1174; Denzinger-Bannwart, *Enchiridion Symbolorum, Definitionum, et Declarationem de rebus Fidei et Morum* (18.-20. ed., Friburgi Brisgoviae: Herder; 1932), n. 85. Henceforth cited Denzinger.

[27] Canon 7—Mansi, II, 1175.

[28] Mansi, IV, 1138-1142; Hefele-Clark, III, 47.

[29] "Huic sanctae fidei omnes consentire convenit. Continet enim pietatem et quae sufficient ad totius orbis utilitatem."—Mansi, IV, 1342 E, 1343.

this is the faith of the Apostles; we all believe thus; the orthodox believe thus".[30] The profession of faith adopted in the fifth session of this council declared:

> . . . the holy and oecumenical council decrees that no one shall advance or write down or encourage another faith, or teach it to others; and if those who, passing over from heathenism or Judaism, or from any heresy, give another faith or creed, if they are Bishops or clerics, they shall be deposed . . . if laymen, excommunicated.[31]

From the foregoing, it can be seen that in the early centuries, the primary concern of the Church regarding the faith was that it be professed by those receiving Baptism, or by those who returned to the fold from heresy. The laws enacted, therefore, were for the most part liturgical.

The development of this attitude can be studied by a perusal of the decrees of the particular councils held in the first five centuries of the Church's existence. For although the legislation of such councils was limited in scope, there can be no doubt that the legal outlook of the universal Church was to a great extent influenced by such legislation, since even the decrees of the particular councils were included in the very early canonical collections.[32]

The Synod of Neocaesarea (314) made the liturgical rule that in the question of the Baptism of catechumens, each must profess his own willingness to enter the Church by a confession of faith.[33] At a plenary council held in Arles in France during the Pontificate of Pope St. Sylvester (314-335) the following was directed at the Donatist heretics who wished to return to the faith:

> De afris, quod propria sua lege utuntur, ut rebaptizent, placuit, ut si ad ecclesiam aliquis de haeresi venerit, interrogent eum symbolum. . . .[34]

[30] Op. cit., III, 316-317; Mansi, VI, 951-955; Hardouin, *Acta Conciliorum et Epistolae Decretales ac Constitutiones Summorum Pontificium* (12 vols., Parisiis, 1715), II, 286-288. Henceforth to be identified by citing editor's name.

[31] Author's translation. Cf. Mansi, VI, 115D-118A; Hefele-Clark, III, 349.

[32] Cf. Cicognani, *Canon Law* (2. ed., Philadelphia: Dolphin Press, 1935), pp. 192-199.

[33] Canon 6—Mansi, II, 541; Hafele-Clark, I, 226.

[34] Canon 8—Denzinger, n. 53; Mansi, II, 472; Hardouin, I, 265.

The Antipriscillian Creed, also called the "Faith of Damasus," was drawn up at a council held in Saragossa in Spain in 380 and sent to the then reigning Pontiff for approval, indicating that even at this early date it was not unusual to send a profession of faith to the Pope as an integral procedure of a council.[85]

The Council of Laodicea (343-381) enacted three canons that are of interest in the consideration of the profession of faith. The first decreed that heretics returning from the Novatian, Photian, or Quartodeciman heresies should not be received into the Church until they anathematized all heresies and learned the Creed.[86] The second ruled that Bishops must be appointed for the government of the Church by the decision of the Metropolitan and of the other Bishops, after they (the Episcopal candidates) had given sufficient proof of their orthodoxy.[87] As it is manifestly impossible for one to give external evidence of what one believes without professing his faith in some manner, it does not seem improbable that a canonical profession of faith was demanded of Episcopal candidates by the examining Bishops as early as the period of this council. It is probable that the council is here demanding that this "examination into the faith" of the candidates be made a part of the permanent procedure in Episcopal elections. Another canon of the same council ruled that those to be baptized should learn the Creed by heart and recite it on Thursday before the Bishop and the priests.[88] It is not known whether "Thursday" referred to by the canon meant the fifth day of Holy Week or every Thursday during the period of instruction. Greek commentators on the council are in favor of the latter interpretation.[89]

What may well be additional legislation regarding the necessity of a profession of faith of some sort by the clergy before ordination is

[85] Denzinger, n. 15, nota 1.

[86] Canon 7—Mansi, II, 565 B.

[87] "Ut episcopi metropolitanorum et eorum qui sunt circumcirca episcoporum judicio in ecclesiastico magistratu constituentur diu examinati et in *ratione fidei* et in rectae rationis dispensatione."—Canon 12—Mansi, II, 565. The Dionysian collection words the canon somewhat differently: "Ut episcopi judicio metropolitanorum et eorum episcoporum qui circumcirca sunt provehantur ad ecclesiasticam potestatem, hi videlicet qui plurimo tempore probantur tam verbo fidei quam rectae conversationis exemplo."—*Op. cit.,* 578. Pseudo-Isidore changes the wording thus: ". . . . et nihilominus in sermone fidei . . . fuerint probati."—*Op. cit.,* 586.

[88] Canon 46—Mansi, II, 572 C.

[89] Hefele-Clark, II, 319.

found in the canons of a synod held in Hippo Regius in Africa in 393. This synod ruled that no one was to be ordained who had not been approved, either by examination or by the testimony of the people.[40] Here again, it is not improbable that a profession of faith formed a part of this "examination." This, it must be remembered, was the time of great heresies, which at that period had startling growth both in Asia and Africa. Not only were the lay people led away from the true Church by the specious arguments of the false leaders, but even the clergy, high and low. In order that the true faith be preserved, therefore, at its very fountainhead, it is only reasonable to suppose that those about to be ordained were required to profess the orthodox Creed, that of Nicaea. Even in the event that a candidate was ordained without examination, on the strength of the "testimony of the people," it must be presumed that he had established his orthodoxy in the eyes of the latter by words and actions that were equivalent to a profession of faith.

In a collection of African ecclesiastical legislation, ascribed by Pseudo-Isidore to the IV Council of Carthage in 398, are two canons of considerable importance. The first decreed that the one who was to be ordained a Bishop must first be examined, above all whether he openly acknowledged the chief points of the faith.[41] The council also ruled that the Bishop was not to ordain anyone without the advice of his clergy and was bound to seek testimony as to the *faith,* morals, etc., of the candidate.[42]

These regulations, directly legislating a canonical profession of faith, are of particular importance. Since the African canons were used in the Spanish collections of ecclesiastical laws,[43] is is likely that the injunction about the examination of those to be ordained served as an example for the similar legislation that is found in the Spanish collections.

At a synod convoked at Constantinople in 448 by Flavian, Ordinary of that See, there were read examples of the orthodox faith, namely, the second letter of Cyril to Nestorius, the approval given this epistle

[40] Canon 20—Mansi, III, 922 B.

[41] Canon 1—Mansi, III, 949 E. According to Hefele, these canons are certainly very old, but the inscription ascribing them to a Carthaginian synod of 398 is spurious. Cf. Hefele-Clark, II, 409.

[42] Canon 22—Mansi, III, 953 A.

[43] Cf. Van Hove, *Commentarium Lovaniense in Codicem Iuris Canonici* (I, *Prolegomena,* Mechliniae-Romae: H. Dessain, 1928), I, 114, n. 128. Hereafter this work will be cited by the use of the word *Prolegomena.*

at the Council of Ephesus, and the letter of Cyril to John of Antioch (containing a new formula of profession of faith for the Oriental Bishops). Flavian required that everyone present at the synod should assent to these declarations of the faith as explaining the true sense of the Nicene Creed.[44]

The Bishops of Africa met in 535 after the Emperor Justinian had put to an end the Vandal kingdom, under which Arianism had flourished. Those present at the council debated whether those who had been Arian priests should, *after making a profession of faith,* be admitted to the clerical ranks, or should be admitted only into lay membership in the Church. They finally decided to ask the then reigning Pontiff, John I, what to do.[45] At a synod held in Asia Minor in 536 several Oriental Bishops asked Pope Agapetus to give one Anthimus, a Bishop, a period of time within which he could clear himself of the suspicion of heresy by means of a profession of faith.[46]

One of the canons, the number of which is unknown, of a council held in Autun in France in 670 ruled that a cleric who refused to profess the faith should be condemned by his Bishop.[47] At about the same time (680) at a council held in Rome, Pope St. Agatho (678-681) ordered the Bishops of Britain to get proof of the orthodox faith of those in the Saxon provinces of their country,[48] a procedure that would be almost impossible unless the Britons of the provinces in question either made a public profession or denial of the faith or subscribed or refused to subscribe to a written confession of the dogmas of the Church.

One thing required by all the Councils of Toledo, held from the beginning of the fifth century to the ninth century, was profession of faith made at some time during the council, showing that this practice had by the fifth century spread into Spain.[49]

[44] Cf. Hefele-Clark, III, 190, 191; Mansi, VI, 679.

[45] Cf. Mansi, VIII, 808; Hefele-Clark, IV, 188.

[46] Cf. Mansi, VIII, 888 C D E, 889 A B; Hefele-Clark, IV, 193.

[47] "Si quis presbyter, diaconus, subdiaconus, vel clericus symbolum quod inspirante Spiritu Sancto Apostoli tradiderunt et fidem Sancti Athanasii praesulis irreprehensibiliter non recensuerit, ab episcopo condemnetur."—Mansi, XI, 125.

[48] Cf. Mansi, XI, 181 D.

[49] Hinschius, *Decretales Pseudo-Isidore et Capitula Angilramni,* pp. 351, 354, 358, 364, 376, 385 et seq., 404-407, 413.

The XI Council of Toledo (675), moreover, is of the utmost importance in the consideration of the legislation concerning the canonical profession of faith to be taken by clerics before ordination. It is this council that introduced for the first time in any ecclesiastical legislation a specific law governing the promise to keep the faith, made by clerics. One of the canons rules that every cleric must before his ordination promise that he will hold fast to the Catholic faith.[50] Although this legislation does not actually demand a profession of faith, it does rule that a promise be made publicly that the faith which one professes exteriorly will be constantly preserved. There is but a minor distinction, one of form only, between this and the formal profession of faith that clerics of today must make.[51] Since the *Collectio Hispana* incorporated the canons of the Councils of Toledo and was in turn the basis of many other collections of canons and decretals, including the famous Pseudo-Isidore, [52] this legislation was soon broadcast throughout Europe and was generally observed.

The Trullan Council, held in Constantinople in 691, repeated the liturgical legislation of prior councils regarding the profession of faith to be made by those about to be baptized.[53] What might be an instruction regarding the confession of faith demanded of those to be consecrated Bishops is to be found in a collection of Irish canons dated about the year 693. In the latter is to be found the following:

> Qui episcopus ordinatus est ante examinetur—si in lege Domini instructus . . .[54]

A council held in Cloveshoe in England in 745 speaks of the examination into the faith of those who were to be ordained.[55] The first Council

[50] Canon 10—Mansi, XI, 143; Hardouin, III, 1028; Hinschius (*Pseudo-Isidorianae et Capitula Angilramni*, p. 410) records the legislation as follows: "Placuit huic sancto concilio ut unisquisque qui ad ecclesiasticos gradus est accessurus non ante honoris consecrationem accipiat quam placiti sui innodatione promittat ut fidem Catholicam sincera cordis devotione custodiens, juste et pie vivere debet."

[51] Cf. Wernz, *Ius Decretalium*, III, n. 13; Benedict XIV, *De Synodo Diocesesana*, lib. V, cap. III, n. 10.

[52] Fournier-Le Bras, *Histoire des Collections Canoniques en Occident* (2 vols., Paris: Recueil Sirey, 1931), I, 171 et seq.; Cicognani, *Canon Law*, p. 239, n. 54; 219, n. 39.

[53] "Quod oportet eos qui illuminantur fidem discere et quinta Septimane feria episcopo seu presbyteris renunciare."—Canon 47—Mansi, XI, 978.

[54] Ch. VII, *De Episcopo*—Mansi, XII, 118.

[55] Canon 6—Mansi, XII, 397.

of Toulon in France, held in 859, also treats of the examination of those to be ordained and ruled that they must be proved in faith and example.[56]

Though the foregoing are somewhat scattered instances, they are sufficient evidence of the practice of the liturgical profession of faith required of those to be baptized and those returning to the faith in the first five centuries of the Christian era. They, moreover, show the beginning of the canonical legislation that required Bishops and priests to make a profession of faith before assuming office, legislation that is recognized to this day and incorporated into the Code of the Canon Law.[57]

Article III. Roman Law Legislation

The official religion of Rome had practically nothing to do with conscience and inner conviction. The religious worship of the Roman State consisted in the precise performance of an external rite. The Roman gods were honored; had to be honored. Because the external act of sacrifice was demanded of all, the vaunted religious toleration of the Roman State was essentially and fundamentally bound up with oppression of conscience for those whose convictions forbade them to perform that external act of sacrifice. Such, above all, were the Christians. [58] Because of this attitude, the Roman State for several centuries after the promulgation of Christianity did not concern itself with the doctrines of the new sect, but with the question: Does the religion of the Christians harmonize with the existence of the State? [59]

It is wrong, however, to look upon the Roman Empire as a bloody persecutor of Christianity. Because it was an eminently rational government, because of its quasi-toleration of all sorts of religious sects and its specific toleration of the Jewish form of worship, it was a fertile field for the spread of the Gospel. The example of its unity

[56] Mansi, XV, 538 E-539. It should be noted that this is but a repetition, as is the legislation of many of the conciliar laws that have been cited, of canon 12 of the Council of Laodicea, mentioned in the Collection of Dionysius. —Mansi, II, 578. The Council of Toulon also ruled thus: ". . . qui ad sacerdotium provocantur judicium sit episcoporus ut ipsi cum qui ordinatus est probent si in fide . . . edoctus sit."—Mansi, *ibid.*

[57] Cf. can. 1406, § 1, 3°, 7°.

[58] Cf. Lortz-Kaiser, *History of the Church* (Milwaukee: Bruce, 1938), p. 28.

[59] *Op. cit.*, p. 29.

of organization was utilized to the fullest by the early Church in its founding of dioceses and ecclesiastical provinces.

The rapid growth of Christianity in the Roman Empire, however, particularly at Rome, had its inevitable results. The paganism of Rome clashed with the doctrines of Christianity, and the persecutions resulted. It would be wrong to accuse the Empire of being stupidly barbarous in its treatment of the Church and its followers. Since the Roman State was pre-eminently legalistic, the Christians' refusal to pay honor to the state-recognized deities was looked upon as contrary to the public good and was, therefore, punishable by penal action.[60]

The persecutions were never constant. They were waged in severity in some provinces and were merely proclaimed in others. Succeeding Emperors were harsh or lenient with the Christians as the exigencies of the times demanded. Before the fourth century, the Church had emerged as the victor of the conflict and the Edict of Milan, issued by Constantine in 313, marked the beginning of the recognition of the Church as a legal society.

As early as 324, Constantine expressed the hope that all his subjects would renounce the heathen superstition and profess the Christian faith.[61] And although paganism was still legally recognized, its influence was dead, and Christianity began to make its influence felt in Roman legislation. The Emperors after Constantine, except Julian the Apostate, withdrew the support of the state from paganism and more and more gave approval to Christianity and the Church.

A. *Theodosian Law*

Julian the Apostate (d. 363) led paganism in a brief revival before its final demise, but Christianity made great strides under Gratian (d. 383) in the West and reached its ultimate triumph in 380, when the Emperor Theodosius (364-395) issued his famous decree ordering all of his subjects to profess the Catholic faith.[62]

[60] *Op. cit.*, pp. 46, 47.

[61] *Op. cit.*, p. 79.

[62] "Cunctos populos quos clementiae nostrae temperamentum in tali volumus religione versari quam Divinum Petrum Apostolum tradidisse Romanis religio usque ad nunc ab ipso insinuata declarat . . . hoc est ut secundum apostolicam disciplinam evangelicamque doctrinam Patris, et Filii, et Spiritus Sancti unam deitatem sub parili maiestate et sub pia trinitate credamus."—C. Th. (16. 1) 1, 2, *Codex Theodosianus* (3 vols., ed. P. Krueger, Th. Mommsen, P. M. Meyer, Berlin, 1905); cf. Lortz-Kaiser, *op. cit.*, p. 86.

This decree, which bore the names of the Emperors Gratian, Valentinian, and Theodosius, was effective in the Eastern as well as the Western Roman Empire; it rang the death knell for paganism, although at the time it was issued one-half of the people of the Empire were still pagans.[63]

Theodosius II sent the tribune Aristolaus to the East to bring to all the Bishops of that region a positive acceptance of the anathema on the heretic Nestorius. To facilitate the work of the tribune, St. Cyril of Alexandria sent to him a declaration of faith to which the Oriental Bishops should be required to subscribe.[64]

The same Emperor in an imperial edict (449) which preceded the actual opening of the Ephesine or Robber synod expressed a wish that all who should desire to add anything to the Nicene confession of faith, or take anything away from it, should not be heeded in the synod.[65]

In 450 the Emperor demanded that Flavian, the newly elected Bishop of Constantinople, make a profession of faith before assuming office.[66]

The Council of Chalcedon was held in 451 under the auspices of the Emperor Marcian. On Feb. 7, 452, the Emperor formally approved the formula of faith subscribed by the fathers of that assembly. He threatened all, clergy, soldiers, and laity, with severe penalties if they should again stir up controversies concerning the faith.[67]

In a second edict on March 13, 452, Marcian declared that the Council of Chalcedon, in agreement with the declarations of faith of the Councils of Nicaea, Constantinople, and Ephesus, had rejected the heresy of Eutyches and had confirmed the truth faith.[68]

There can be no doubt that by the middle of the fifth century, Roman law, as evidenced by the decrees of the Emperors, was definitely on the side of orthodoxy and that the Emperors considered themselves

[63] Lortz-Kaiser, *op. cit.*, p. 83.

[64] Cf. Mansi, V, 967.

[65] Cf. Hefele-Clark, III, 224; Mansi, VI, 600; Hardouin, II, 80.

66 Cf. Hefele-Clark, III, 211; Mansi, VI, 539; Hardouin, II, 7.

[67] Cf. Hefele-Clark, III, 438-439; "Ordinatis itaque religiose et fideliter quae venerandam orthodoxam fidem fundasse noscuntur, ita ut nulla in posterum dubitatio, vel illis qui calumniari divinitatem assolent relinqueretur; sacro nostrae serenitatis edicto venerandam synodum confirmantes, admonuimus universos ut de religione disputare disinerent . . ."—Mansi, VII, 174.

[68] Cf. Mansi, VII, 478; Hefele-Clark, III, 439.

the champions of the faith, which they endeavored to have all their citizens profess either implicitly, by avoidance of heresy, or explicitly, by public profession if the need arose.

B. *Justinian Legislation*

By the time of Justinian (527-565) the legal principle had been evolved that only those persons who had been baptized were capable of possessing full rights. In his Code Justinian re-enacted the legislation of Theodosius, requiring all the citizens of the Empire to profess the Catholic faith.[69]

This is not, it is true, direct legislation to the effect that a formal profession of faith be made by every citizen, but it does entail a public acceptance of the dogmas of the Church as contained in the formularies of faith that were then extant, notably the Apostles' and the Nicene Creeds. Justinian commanded in the same legislation:

> We order all those who follow this law to assume the name of Catholic Christians, and, considering others as demented and insane, we order that they shall bear the infamy of heresy. . . .[70]

Continuing the legislation mentioned above, the Justinian Code further rules, as had Theodosius, Gratian, and Valentinian in a previous age:

> . . . . let the name of the only and greatest God be celebrated everywhere, and let the observance of the Nicene Creed, recently transmitted by our ancestors, and firmly established by the testimony and practice of Divine religion, always remain secure.
>
> We direct that all Catholic churches throughout the entire world shall be placed under the control of the orthodox Bishops who have embraced the Nicene Creed.[71]

That there was a distinct formulary of faith to which the Roman citizens could subscribe is further indicated by the Code of Justinian when it re-enacted the instruction of the Emperor Marcian. In this Marcian said that those things that pertain to the Christian faith had

[69] C. (1. 1) 1, *Corpus Iuris Civilis* (3 vols., ed. Kreuger-Mommsen-Schoell-Kroll, Berolini, 1928-1929); cf. Lortz-Kaiser, *op. cit.*, p. 86.

[70] Author's translation. C. (1. 1) 1.

[71] Author's translation. C. (1. 1) 2.

been settled by the Fathers who had met at Chalcedon and had drawn up a formulary that was in conformity with both the Nicene Creed, the Apostolic explanations, and the decisions of the first Ecumenical Council of Constantinople in 381.[72]

A letter from Pope St. John to Justinian is included in the Code and has the force of law. In this epistle the Pontiff, speaking of the followers of the heretic Cyrus, declared that they should be excluded from communion with the other members of the Church, unless, having renounced their errors, they *made a profession of the true faith* and declared their intention of adhering firmly to it. On the other hand, he asked Justinian to accept these heretics as Catholics if they renounced their errors and wished to return to the bosom of the Church.[73] In the Emperor's letter to the same Pontiff, there was assurance that he (Justinian) would always promote the true faith; that he recognized the teachings of the sacred Councils of Nicaea, Constantinople, Ephesus, and Chalcedon.[74]

In the Justinian Code is also found the earliest record that a profession of faith was demanded of an official of the Episcopal curia. Repeating an edict of the Emperor Anastasius to Eustachius, Praetorian Prefect, the Code ruled:

> We order that only those shall be selected for the office of defender who have been initiated into the mysteries of the orthodox religion and who have established this in the first place by the testimony of their acts and by the proclaiming this belief with the sanction of an oath in the presence of a most reverend Bishop of the Catholic Church. We order that they shall be appointed in this manner and that they shall be confirmed by a decree of the most reverend Bishop, clerks, nobles, and officials of the Curia.[75]

Repeating a decree of the Emperors Gratian, Valentinian, and Theodosius to a Praetorian Prefect in 379, the Justinian Code declared that all those were to be classed as heretics and hence subject to the sanctions of law who had deviated from the judgment and principles of the Catholic religion.[76] This judgment could not be passed and the sanctions inflicted unless there was some sort of profession of

[72] C. (1. 1) 4.

[73] C. (1. 1) 8. 7.

[74] C. (1. 1) 7.

[75] Author's translation. C. (1. 4) 19.

[76] C. (1. 5) 2.

faith to which the suspected person was asked to subscribe, or which he might reject. The same can be said for the legislation which prescribed that the children of Manichean or Donatist heretics could not succeed as heirs, or take possession of their estates unless "they abandon the perverseness of their fathers."[77]

Perhaps the most important enactment of Justinian legislation with regard to civil approbation of purely ecclesiastical laws is the blanket endorsement in the *Novels* of the decrees of the Ecumenical Councils of Nicaea, Constantinople, Ephesus, and Chalcedon. Justinian wrote that he received the religious teachings of these four synods as Sacred Scripture and observed the canons as laws.[78] The importance of this legislation lies in the fact that it gives the sanction of civil law to much of the legislation on the profession of faith that has been considered in the first part of this work.

Justinian at one time in his reign also recommended that the Bishops of his empire sign a profession of faith. The occasion of this was the following incident: There had been a rift between the Church at Constantinople and the Sovereign Pontiff. It had been caused by the inclusion by the Patriarch of Jerusalem of the name of Acacius, one of the opponents of the teachings of the Council of Chalcedon, in the diptychs, or honor roll of saints, that was read at the Divine Service. This rift was finally healed in March, 519, when the Patriarch John of Constantinople signed a libellus or profession of faith sent him by the Pope. In this profession was contained an anathema on several heretics. Observing that an amicable solution of doctrinal difficulties could be produced in such a manner, Justinian suggested that all the Bishops of his kingdom sign the libellus.[79]

In his celebrated edict issued against the heretic Origen, Justinian, moreover, prescribed that no one in the future was to be ordained Bishop or head of a monastery unless he should add to the customary anathema on contemporaneous heretics a special anathema on Origen.[80]

Later Emperors also legislated on the profession of faith, at least indirectly, but the decrees and the laws mentioned in the foregoing comprise the bulk of the Roman law legislation on the subject treated in this thesis.

77 C. (1. 5) 4. 6.

78 N. (131. 1).

79 Cf. Hefele-Clark, III, 122, 123; Mansi, VIII, 451-452.

80 Cf. Mansi, IX, 523; Hefele-Clark, IV, 219.

Article IV. The *Liber Diurnus*

As has been observed previously, at a very early age the Church was compelled to protect herself against heresy by demanding absolute orthodoxy of those who were to be her ministers. Thus it was that the higher ecclesiastics from the fourth century onwards had to subscribe to a special documentary evidence of their faith.[81] According to evidences that are indisputable, the Roman Bishops were the first to establish the custom of making a profession of faith before they assumed their office. This was a natural consequence of the importance of the Primatial See and the place of authority the Roman Pontiffs held in the whole Christian world.[82]

That a set formula of profession of faith was very probably used by the Roman See very early in its existence is indicated by the ancient formularies that were in use at the Apostolic chancery from the sixth to the ninth centuries. The most important of these early formularies is certainly the *Liber Diurnus Romanorum Pontificum,* a collection of 107 formularies, applicable to a large number of functions, which was long used in the Roman Chancery. The *Liber Diurnus* that has come down to us has without doubt copied many of its documents from the *Registrum* or letter book of St. Gregory the Great (590-604). Modern scholarship, moreover, has uncovered some evidences in the formulas themselves that would lead one to believe that many of the formulas are considerably older than the time of Gregory; and that though they had been adapted to the needs of the times as new problems arose, they are fundamentally of very ancient origin.[83] Certainly the actual date of origin of several of the formulas is disputed. Garnier, Baluzius, Zaccaria, De Roziere, and Sickel have conjectured about the probable time, the last two in the light of modern research.[84] It is certain that

[81] Cf. Hinschius, *Das Kirchenrecht der Katholiken und Protestanten in Deutschland,* III, 218; Benedict XIV, *De Synodo Dioecesana,* lib. V, cap. II, n. 9; Wernz, *Ius Decretalium,* III, n. 13.

[82] Cf. Hinschius, *op. cit.,* 219; Wernz, *loc. cit.*

[83] W. Pietz, S.J., writing on "*Liber Diurnus*" (*Sitzungsberichte der Akademie der Wissenschaften in Wien, philos.-histor. Klasse* [Wien, 1847], vol. 185, n. 4, I, 144), declares that many of the formulas of the *Liber Diurnus* are pre-Constantine in their origin, particularly the professions of faith. With considerable acumen he shows that many of the formularies of profession existed before the year 430. Santifaller in an article, "Zur Liber Diurnus-Forschung" *(Historische Zeitschrift* [Munchen und Berlin], vol. 161, pp. 535, sqq.), opposes this theory and would set the origin of the profession formularies at a later date.

[84] Cf. Sickel, "Prolegomena Zum Liber Diurnus I und II," *Sitzungsberichte der Akademie der Wissenschaften in Wien, philos.-hist. Klasse,* vol. 117, VII.

the *Liber Diurnus* we know is not the original one. One of the collections of formularies was compiled in the Pontificate of Hadrian I (772-795), but this is at least the third such collection, the other two certainly having been in existence between the time of Gregory the Great and Hadrian, and possibly even before that time. More formularies were added during the Pontificate of Leo III (795-816) and the collection was in constant use until the Pontificate of Gregory VII (1073-1085).[85]

The value of the *Liber Diurnus* in the consideration of profession of faith is that it contains the formulas of such professions made by the Roman Pontiffs, the Bishops of Italy, and other Bishops from very early times. The diurnal that will be used as the basis of study here is that edited by De Roziere, a critical edition containing the text of the *Liber Diurnus* published by the Jesuit, Garnier, in 1680, with annotations from the texts of Holstenius.[86]

According to Garnier, with the exception of those for the profession of faith, the formularies in his edition of the *Liber Diurnus* were written shortly after 714, but were based on those taken from earlier collections, especially from the day book of Gregory the Great.[87] In his annotations on Garnier's comments about the age of the formularies, Zaccaria declares that the diurnal is as old as the fifth century.[88]

Stephen Baluzius (1630-1718), who also edited a *Liber Diurnus,* says in his preface to the work that some of the formulas go back to

pp. 1-76; XIII, pp. 1-94. "La recherche du temps ou notre collection fut composee souleve une question bien autrement delicate, et nous tomberions dans des embarras inextricables si nous pretendions le determiner avec precision . . . . On n'obtient pas ainsi une date rigoureusement exacte, mais on arrive arestreindre l'incertitude dans des limites assez etroites, seul resultat qu'on puisse legitimement esperer."—De Roziere, *Liber Diurnus ou Recueil des Formules Usitees par la Chancellerie Pontificale du V au XI Siecle* (Paris, 1869), p. xv.

[85] Cf. Van Hove, *Prolegomena,* p. 125-127; Boudinhon, "Formularies," *The Catholic Encyclopaedia* (15 vols., New York, 1907-1912), vol. V; De Roziere, *op. cit.,* pp. xxix, xxx.

[86] Garnier's text and comments are to be found in *MPL,* CV, 1-182.

[87] "Quod autem dixi de formulis, quoad locum unde haustae sunt, non perinde intelligi debet de professionibus fidei aliisque ad ordinationem, tum summi pontificis, tum episcopi pertinentibus; id enim, aut fere totum, aut quoad magnam partem desumptum videtur ex iis quae in ordinatione pontificum paulo post sextam synodum (680) contigerunt; nam professiones fidei a superioribus pontificibus emissae, cum pontificatum capesserent, multum differunt ab iis quas edimus, ut ex collatione patebit."—*MPL,* CV, 3; De Roziere, *op. cit.,* pp. ccxix, ccxx.

88 De Roziere, *op, cit.,* p. ccix, nota 1.

the time of Pope Gelasius (492-496) and Pope Pelagius (556-561).[89] Baluzius' assumption that the formularies containing the profession of faith for the Popes and Bishops were in use as early as the end of the fifth century corroborates the testimony of John the Deacon, who wrote the life of Gregory the Great. This writer declared that Gregory, at the beginning of his Pontificate, had made a profession of faith in which he renounced all heresies, *which practice other Pontiffs, even before that time, had been accustomed to do.*[90]

John distinguished two professions of faith that were made by the Roman Pontiffs, one before consecration, the other afterwards—one made as a private individual about to be elected Pope, the second pronounced as Pope to show the whole world the authentic faith. The first profession was called *Symbolum,* the second, *Synodica.* John tells of Gregory's sending the *Synodica, "secundum priscum decessorum morem suorum,"* to the Patriarchs of Constantinople, Alexandria, Antioch, and Jerusalem.[91]

The *Liber Diurnus* shows that a three-fold profession was used in the seventh, eighth, and ninth centuries in the consecration of a Pope. The one to be elected was led in solemn procession to the tomb of the Apostle, where he made a profession of faith. After his consecration as Bishop of Rome, he made another profession. Finally, he made a profession in his sermon, "urbi et orbi." [92] The formula of profession, of course, changed with the times. In the earliest centuries, the professions made were probably the Apostles' or the Nicene Creeds. Later, as new heresies arose, the need for specific inclusion of points of doctrine was felt. An examination into the intrinsic structure of the professions contained in Garnier's diurnal gives evidence that they are based on earlier formulas. One of the professions mentioned in the *Liber Diurnus* for the consecration of a Pope was revised, as can be seen from internal evidence, between 685 and 715, very probably in

[89] "Sed cum aliquot ex eo formulis usi sint Gelasius et Pelagius istius nominis primi Romani pontifices, non puto posse dubitari quin eorum aevo is liber in usu fuerit. Eo autem usum quoque fuisse sanctum Graegorium liquet ex variis illius epistolis."—De Roziere, *op. cit.,* ccxxxvi. Baluzius' conclusion is probably based on the formulary requiring the profession of faith of Bishops. The words of this formulary are in many parts identical with those of an epistle of Pope Pelagius to Bishop Elias. This gives rise to the presumption that the formula for the profession of faith was used in that day. Cf. De Roziere, *op. cit.,* p. 139.

[90] Cf. Hinschius, *op. cit.,* III, 219, nota 1; Coronata, *Institutiones Iuris Canonici* (5 vols., Romae; Marietti; II, *De Rebus,* 2. ed., 1939), II, 384, n. 967.

[91] Cf. *MPL,* CV, 133.

[92] Cf. *MPL,* CV, 27.

the Pontificate of Pope Gregory II (715-731), for the letter of this Pontiff to the Emperor Leo on the occasion of his consecration as Pope contains virtually the same words that are contained in the profession in the diurnal.[93] The third profession contained in the diurnal, that addressed to the whole Catholic world, is probably, according to Garnier, the work of Pope Leo II and was included in the *Liber Diurnus* at about 682, as it contains phrases and sentences from the writings of that Pontiff.[94] That these formularies are attributed to such a comparatively late age is no argument against the fact that there were earlier formularies of profession. For it is probable that the *Liber Diurnus* underwent a partial revision in the seventh century and a complete revision again in the eighth century.[95]

The *Liber Diurnus* also gives evidence that a profession of faith was demanded of the suburbicarian Bishops of Rome. After one had been nominated or elected by the clergy and people, his name was sent to the Pope together with a request that he be consecrated. If the Pope consented, the consecration was held, *"praevio examine de fide et moribus."* At the consecration ceremony itself the newly created Bishop made a profession of faith at the tomb of St. Peter.[96] The promise of faith taken by these Bishops mentions Pope Martin I, who died in 655, the VI Ecumenical Council (681), and Constantine Pogonatus, who died in 685. Hence it must have been composed or revised before the death of the latter, probably in the early part of the seventh century.[97]

An *"Indiculum Episcopi"* or attestation of faith to be taken by Bishops outside of Italy is also found in the *Liber Diurnus.* The formula in this *indiculum* is the same as that signed by St. Boniface,

[93] Cf. *MPL,* CV, 44, nota "f".

[94] *Ibid.,* 53, nota "c"; 54, nota "e".

[95] Cf. Santifaller, *loc. cit.*

[96] Cf. *MPL,* CV, 59, nota 52.

[97] Garnier holds for the seventh century composition of the profession—*MPL,* CV, 63, 64, notae "c" et "d." Baluzius believes that it is much older than this, probably because it contains portions that are identical with a profession mentioned by Pope Pelagius.—De Roziere, *op. cit.,* p. 136. Peitz would have it much older.—*loc. cit.* The profession is in part as follows: "Promitto ille ego talis, episcopus sanctae ecclesiae illius, domino meo sanctissimo et ter beatissimo illi summo pontifici seu universali papae, et per vos sanctae vestrae catholicae et apostolicae sedi, devota mentis integritate et pura conscientia formoque, ut oportet, proposito, quae pro firmamento sive rectitudine catholicae fidei et orthodoxiae religioni conveniunt, me profiteri. . ."—De Roziere, *op. cit.,* pp. 137-139.

Archbishop of Mainz, when he bound himself to the Apostolic See on the occasion of his consecration as Bishop in 722.[98] Gregory II had written to St. Boniface concerning this profession, ordering that he make it, as did all Bishops at the time of their consecration.[99] In the *Liber Diurnus* is also found the *"Indiculum Episcopi de Langobardia,"* used by the Bishops of Northern Italy. It does not differ radically from the promise demanded by Pope Gregory II from St. Boniface. Both Garnier and Baluzius hold that from internal evidence it can be proved that the profession was in use at the time of Queen Theodelinda (before 626).[100]

From the evidence contained in the *Liber Diurnus* one can conclude, therefore, that the practice of the Roman Pontiffs of making a profession of faith was constant from the fifth to the eighth centuries, possibly earlier. How long the Roman Pontiffs continued this practice is not definitely known. In the interval from the eighth century to the time of Boniface VIII (1294), there is no more evidence for the existence of the practice than the fact that the diurnal was in constant use until the eleventh century.[101] The value of the *Liber Diurnus* as a testimony to the existence of the practice of profession of faith by the Bishops of the Church is also evident. The fact that the *Liber Diurnus* is cited both by Ivo of Chartres [102] and Gratian [103] is merely an indication that the work was recognized as a canonical source by the collectors of the tenth and eleventh centuries.

After the profession of faith taken by Boniface VIII, which is unlike the profession in the diurnal in many parts and which contains, in addition, a promise to protect the possessions of the Church, there is no evidence that the Pontiffs continued the practice. This is not in-

[98] "Promitto . . . me omnem fidem et puritatem sanctae fidei catholicae exhibere et in unitate eiusdem fidei Deo operante persistere. . . ."—Mansi, XII, 235; De Roziere, *op. cit.*, pp. 157-160.

[99] Cf. Benedict XIV, *De Synodo Dioecesana,* lib. V. cap. III, n. 10; Mansi, *op. cit.*, 235.

[100] Cf. De Roziere, *op. cit.*, p. 160.

[101] Cf. Santifaller, *op. cit.*, p. 536. Hinschius says that it was discontinued after the eighth century until the time of Boniface VIII.—Cf. *Das Kirchenrecht der Katholiken und Protestanten in Deutschland,* III, 219. But there is no evidence to support this theory other than that the profession of the Pontiffs is not mentioned.

[102] *Decretum,* IV, 132—*MPL,* CLXI, 296; *Panormia,* II, 103—*MPL, op. cit.*, 1107.

[103] C. 8, D. XVI.

dicative, of course, that the custom was not in use, but it must have been discontinued before the Councils of Constance (1414) and Basle (1436), for both of them legislated that the Popes should make a profession of faith before their election was made public.[104]

Article V. Papal Decretals and Other Evidences of the Period

The Popes from the fifth to the eighth centuries made strenuous efforts to check the growth of heresy and to preserve orthodoxy in the whole Christian world. It was their custom to demand a written profession of faith from Bishops and clerics whenever there arose a question of faith,[105] or when dogmas were defined to combat the teachings of the heretics. A few examples of this Papal vigilance over the faith of both clergy and people is important in the consideration of the history of the profession of faith.

Pope Martin I wrote in 649 to one John, Bishop of Philadelphia near Jerusalem, Papal Vicar in the East, exhorting him to effect a reconciliation with those clerics who had been deposed because of their lack of orthodoxy. He instructed the Bishop to reinstate those clerics in their offices provided they signed a written confession of the orthodox faith.[106] In an encyclical letter addressed to all the faithful of the Patriarchates of Jerusalem and Antioch, the same Pontiff set forth the decrees of the I Lateran Synod (650) and required that they make a profession of these decrees as orthodox doctrine.[107] Another Pope of the same period, Leo II, after confirming the acts of the VI Ecumenical Council (680), immediately began to promulgate them throughout the West. In letters to the Bishops of Spain he ordered

[104] Cf. De Roziere, *op. cit.*, p. 311. The reason for the legislation lies in the fact that there was a very strong movement against the Primacy of the Pope evident at both councils.—Cf. Hardouin, III, 1202. A discussion of the anti-Papacy tendency of both the councils may be found in Schroeder's *Disciplinary Decrees of the General Councils*, pp. 443-452, and 456-474.

[105] Cf. Mansi, VI, 83-84, for the demand of Pope Leo I that Anatolius make a profession of faith before the Pontiff would confirm his appointment as Patriarch of Constantinople.

[106] Cf. Jaffe, *Regesta Pontificum Romanorum ab Condita Ecclesia ad annum post Christum natum MCXCVIII* (2 vols. in 1, Lipsiae, 1885-1888), n. 2064. Future references to this work will be made by citing only the author's name. Cf. Mansi, X, 810 C.

[107] Cf. Mansi, X, 827; Hefele-Clark, V, 117-118; Jaffe, n. 2070. A request for a universal profession of faith is contained in a letter of this Pontiff to all Christendom.—Cf. Mansi, X, 1176 E-1178 A; Hefele-Clark, V, 114-115.

that the decrees of this Council be received and subscribed.[108] It has been indicated that, at a synod held in Rome in 680, Pope Agatho requested that the Bishops of Britain get proof of the orthodox faith of those in the Saxon provinces. Eight years later Theodore, Archbishop of Canterbury, wrote this report:

> Licentiam non habemus Britonibus petentibus chrisma vel Eucharistiam dare nisi ante confessi fuerint se nobiscum esse in unitate ecclesiae . . .[109]

At a chapter held for his priests in 852, Hincmar, Archbishop of Rheims, ruled as follows:

> Ut unusquisque presbyterorum expositionem symboli . . . juxta traditionem orthodoxorum patrum discat . . . Nec non et sermonem Athenasii et fide . . . memoriae quisque commendet . . . et verbis communibus enuntiare queat.[110]

At a chapter held in Orleans in France in 871 under the leadership of Bishop Walter it was ordered that the archdeacons inquire into the faith of the priests in the parishes so that a judgment could be made as to the priests' orthodoxy.[111]

The *Capitula Regum Francorum* contain specific legislation on profession of faith. The following decree, taken from a German synod held about 744, at which Boniface was Papal legate, is repeated in the "Liber Septimus" of the *Capitularium Karoli Magni et Ludovici Pii:*

> Quando presbyteri vel diaconi per parochi constituuntur oportet eos Episcopo suo professionem facere.[112]

The *Capitula* also state that those who acted contrary to this profession were to be deposed.[113]

[108] Cf. Hefele-Clark, V, 181; Mansi, XI, 1050 E-1053 B; Jaffe, n. 2119.

[109] Mansi, XII, 33.

[110] Mansi, XV, 475 D. In his formularies on the Episcopate, Jacob Sirmond, who wrote his work in 1623, mentions a profession of faith made to Hincmar by one of his Suffragan Bishops. He also indicates a general profession to be taken by one elected to the Archbishopric.—Cf. Mansi, XVIII B, 616.

[111] "Ut per archdiaconos vita, intellectus, et doctrina cardinalium presbyterorum investigatur."—Mansi, XV, 504 E-505 A.

[112] Can. 10—Mansi, XVII B, 154; can. 466—Mansi, XVII B, 1129. According to the best critical research, "Liber Septimus" is a spurious collection, but it does at least give evidence of a comparatively early recognition of legislation on profession of faith.

[113] "Qui contra professionem vel subscriptionem suam venerit, in concilio deponatur."—Can. 304, "Liber Sextus"; can. 158, "Liber Septimus."—Mansi, XVII B, 975, 1059.

At a council held under Pope Hadrian I, it was ordered that the Bishops of each church examine the priests at the yearly synods as to their faith, so that the Apostolic faith might be confessed by all.[114] At the III Council of Valencia, held under the auspices of Pope Leo IV in 855, a canon on the election of Bishops ruled that the candidate should be examined as to the probity of his life and the extent of his knowledge. It declared that the Metropolitan should see to it that the candidate be not tainted with simonical heresy. Again, it is not too much to suppose that this examination entailed a profession of faith.[115]

Worth consideration also is the legislation of a council held in Toulouse in 1129, for it demanded that every male over 14 and every female over 12 abjure all heresy and swear that he or she would always follow the faith of the Roman Catholic Church.[116]

[114] ". . . ut sancta et inviolata fides Nicaeni concilii ab omnibus qui sacro cultui mancipantur, fideliter et firmiter teneatur et ab omni anno in synodalibus conventibus ab episcopis singularum ecclesiarum presbyteri . . . de ipsa fide diligentissime examinentur, ita ut apostolicam fidem . . . sicut tradita est nobis a sancta Romana ecclesia per omnia confiteantur . . ."—Mansi, XII, 939.

[115] Canon 7—Mansi, XV, 7.

[116] "Universi tam mares quam feminae, masculi a XIV anno et supra, feminae a XII abjurent omnem haeresem extollentem se adversus sanctam et Catholicam ecclesiam, et fidem orthodoxam quibuscumque nominibus censeatur; jurent etiam quod fidem catholicam quam Romana ecclesia tenet et praedicat, servabunt et haereticos pro viribus persequentur et eos bona fide manifestabunt." —Hardouin, VI [2], 1151.

CHAPTER II

PROFESSION OF FAITH IN THE MIDDLE AGES

ARTICLE I. EVIDENCES FROM GRATIAN'S DECRETUM

The collection compiled by the Camaldulese monk, Gratian, in the year 1140[1] and called by him *Concordia Discordantium Canonum, Nova Collectio, Corpus Iuris Canonici,* but more commonly known as the *Decretum,* is of great value in the consideration of the topic being treated. Because the *Decretum* was by far the most scientific compilation made of canon law up to the twelfth century and because it immediately became the most influential work in the jurisprudence of the Church, it seemed almost at once to become the prevailing canon law.[2] But in spite of the enthusiastic reception of the *Decretum* by Churchmen and canonists alike and notwithstanding the fact that it was cited by both Pope and Ecumenical Council, it was never approved as an authentic collection.[3] Hence the authority it possesses is no more or less than the authority of the sources it uses. A decree it cites from an Ecumenical Council has the force of universal law; a canon taken from a particular council has no added force by reason of being included by Gratian in his collection; a law taken from the decretals of the Popes and included in the *Decretum* has only the force that the Pontiff who issued it intended. It must be remembered, however, that Gratian compiled the sources of the laws then observed in Europe; that many of the laws contained in the *Decretum,* because of the great influence they exerted on later compilers of authentic collections, became the law that eventually found its way into the present Code of Canon Law.[4]

[1] Cf. Kuttner, "The Father of the Science of Canon Law," *The Jurist* (The School of Canon Law, Catholic University of America, Washington, D. C., 1941), I, 3-19.

[2] Cf. Van Hove, *Prolegomena,* p. 160, 161; *Augustine,* A Commentary on the *New Code of Canon Law* (I, 6. ed., St. Louis: Herder, 1931), I, 34; Cicognani, *Canon Law,* p. 281.

[3] "Without being an official collection, and notwithstanding its merely private authority, it became the generally accepted digest of ecclesiastical laws, was copied in innumerable manuscripts (of which still some hundreds are preserved), consulted in the courts, explained and annotated in the rising schools."—Kuttner, *loc. cit.*

[4] Cf. Cicognani, *op. cit.,* p. 288; Augustine, *op. cit.,* 34.

In view of the foregoing, it is necessary to consider the legislation concerning the question of the profession of faith contained in the *Decretum* and to see what canons and decrees pertaining to the subject were considered important enough by Gratian to be included into his collection. The fact that he included canons on the profession of faith argues that they were regarded as obligatory in his day. Many of the laws and canons he cites have been considered in previous chapters of this work. Some of the legislation contained in the *Decretum* will be considered here for the first time, not because it is original with Gratian, but because it is contained in decrees of Popes and councils that have not been treated heretofore in this dissertation.

The *Decretum* repeated the following canons and decretals that already have been considered:

The important tenth canon of the XI Council of Toledo, which legislated that no one was to be ordained unless he promised to serve well and retain the faith that he possessed.[5] The canon from the IV Council of Carthage which ruled that no one was to be ordained unless he had been previously examined by the ordaining Bishop or endorsed by the populace (which examination might well have included the demand that the candidate make a profession of faith, as has been discussed in a previous chapter).[6] The rule of the twelfth canon of the Council of Laodicea, repeated in the seventh canon of the council held in Orleans in France in 871 and several other particular councils, that it was the duty of the Metropolitans and the Bishops to examine all candidates for the Episcopal dignity as to their faith.[7] The earliest recorded legislation regarding the examination of the clergy before ordination, that contained in the ninth canon of I Nicaea.[8] The eighth canon of the same council, which demanded that converts from the Novatian heresy must make a profession of faith before being received into the Church.[9]

Gratian also noted the following canonical legislation on profession of faith that has not been considered before in this dissertation:

A decree of Pope Nicholas II (1059-1061) in a council held in Rome in 1060 requiring that those who were to be ordained Bishops

[5] C. 5, D. XXIII. All quotations from the Decretum are from *Corpus Iuris Canonici* (2 vols., ed. Lipsiensis 2, Post A. L. Richter—Friedburg, Lipsiae, 1928)

[6] C. 2, D. XXIV.

[7] C. 4, D. XXIV.

[8] C. 4, D. LXXXI. A repetition of this legislation as given at a Roman Council under Pope Martin I is contained in C. 7, D. XXIV.

[9] C. 8, C. I, q. 7.

must first be examined, particularly to see whether they assented by a given verbal formula to the documents of faith.[10] This is indeed valuable legislation in the consideration of the topic under discussion, for it shows that at least in Rome the *examination* of candidates before they were consecrated Bishops included the demand that a profession of faith be made. That the other specific demands for "examination" in decrees that have been cited in this work also mean that a profession of faith was asked of the candidate for ordination is rendered by this token the more probable. Certainly the commentators on Gratian's *Decretum* thought so, for they invariably cite in their discussion of such professions the canons already mentioned in this chapter.

The ruling of Pope John VIII (872-882) that he would not confer the pallium on Willbert, Archbishop of Cologne, because in the latter's profession of faith was not contained all that was required.[11]

A warning of Pope Pelagius to the Metropolitans (also expressed in a council held in Ravenna in 877) that if they did not follow the *sanctioned custom* and send within three months a profession of faith to the Apostolic See, they would be deprived of their dignity.[12]

The *Decretum* also cited several liturgical decrees concerning the profession of faith to be taken by those heretics who wish to enter the Church. The following are examples:

St. Cyril of Alexandria in a letter to one of the Bishops of his province declared that the Donatists and Novatians should not be ordained; but if they had been ordained they should manifest their faith by letter to Him He also demanded that one Donatus, who was a convert with his flock from the Novatian sect, send him a written denial of the Novatian doctrine and a profession of the orthodox faith.[13] The author of the *Decretum* also included another letter from St. Cyril ruling that all priests, deacons, subdeacons, and all clerics who wished to return to the Catholic faith must first make an abjuration of their heresy and then a public profession of the orthodox faith.[14]

[10] C. 2, D. XXIII.

[11] "Optatum tibi pallium nunc conferre nequivimus quia fidei tuae paginam minus quam oportet continere reperimus, cum videlicet nullam in ea sanctarum universalum sindorum, in quibus fidei nostrae symbolum continetur, nec decretalium pontificum Romanorum constitutorum, *secundum morem feceris mentionem,* sed nec illam propria subscriptione munieries, nec aliquem qui hanc jurejurando firmaret miseras."—C. 4, D. C; Mansi, XVII A, 242 C.

[12] C. 1, D. C; cf. Mansi, XVII A, 337 C.

[13] C. 19 and 20, C. I, q. 7.

[14] C. 21, C. I. q. 7.

The following is attributed by Gratian to Pope Martin I:

> Si quis episcopus, alicuius episcopi presbyter aut diaconus in alicuius haeresis opinionem offenderit, et ob hanc causam fuerit excommunicatus, nullus episcopus in communionem eum recipiat nisi prius in communi concilio porrecto fidei suae libello satisfaciat omnibus . . .[15]

The author of the *Decretum* also treated of the liturgical profession of faith that must be taken before one received Baptism, citing as his authority many of the canons of the councils that have been noticed earlier in this work,[16] and also some of the early Fathers.[17] He also included the profession of faith made by the Roman Pontiffs and contained in the *Liber Diurnus*.[18] He noted, too, the repudiation of heresy and the profession of faith and oath of allegiance made by Berengarius of Tours (1088) at a synod held in Rome during the Pontificate of Gregory VII.[19]

The following legislation of a council held in Montpellier in France in 506 was also included in the *Decretum:*

> Symbolum etiam placuit ab omnibus ecclesiis una die, i.e., ante octo dies dominicae resurrectionis, publice in ecclesia competentibus praedicari.[20]

In the century that elapsed between Gratian and the appearance of the Decretals of Pope Gregory IX, compiled by St. Raymond of Pennafort from existing collections and promulgated in 1234, there was an increase in ecclesiastical legislation. But the exigencies of the time did not seem to demand that many laws be issued by Pontiff or council regarding the profession of faith.

[15] C. 22, C. I, q. 7. This, according to the Richter-Friedburg edition of the *Corpus Iuris canonici,* is merely an interpretation of canon 8 of the Council of Nicaea.

[16] Cf. C. 74, D. IV, *de cons.;* c. 73, D. IV, *de cons.*

[17] Cf. c. 30, D. III, *de cons.;* cc. 39, 40, D. V, *de cons.*

[18] C. 8, D. XVI.

[19] C. 42, D. II, *de cons;* Mansi, XX, 524 D; Hardouin, VI, 1585; Denzinger, n. 355. The adjuration and profession is in part as follows: "Ego, Berengarius, indignus ecclesiae S. Mauritii Andegauensis diaconus . . . anathematizo omnem haeresim . . . Consentio autem sanctae Romanae ecclesiae et Apostolicae Sedi et ore et corde profiteor . . ."

[20] C. 56, D. IV, *de cons.*

In the *Quinque Compilationes Antiquae,* the five important collections of Papal decretals made in the period from 1140 to 1230,[21] but few references are made to the subject under discussion. In the article on the Decretals of Gregory IX, the source of the legislation included by that Pontiff will be indicated as one or another of these five collections.

Article II. Other Evidences of the Gratian Period

There is evidence of the practice of making the profession of faith at councils from the acts of the Council of Rheims (1140.)[22] It is known that Pope Innocent III (1198-1216) in an encyclical, *Eius exemplo,* of Dec. 18, 1208, prescribed a profession of faith to be taken by Durand of Huesca and his Waldensian companions.[23] The XII Ecumenical Council (IV Lateran), convoked in 1215 by Pope Innocent III to combat the Albigensians, the followers of the Abbot Joachim, and the Waldensians, issued a profession of faith that contradicted the errors of the day.[24] As was the custom, the acts, including the new profession of faith, were presented to the assembled Bishops and clergy for acceptance.[25]

Article III. The Decretals of Gregory IX

As has been indicated, only a few enactments regarding profession of faith are to be found in the decretals of Pope Gregory IX. The reason for this is to be found in the rather obvious fact that the Popes evidently did not see the need for additional laws on the subject. The necessary legislation was for the most part contained in the *Decretum.*

[21] Cf. Friedburg, *Quinque Compilationes Antiquae* (Leipsic, 1882); *Augustinius, Antiquae Decretalium Collectiones Commentariis et Emendationibus Illustratae* (Parisiis, 1621).

[22] Cf. Mansi, XXI, 725; Denzinger, n. 389; Hardouin, VI, 1309.

[23] Cf. Denzinger, n. 420; Potthast, *Regesta Romanorum Pontificum inde ab a. p. Chr. 1198 ad a. 1304* (2 vols., Berolini, 1874-1875), n. 3571. This formula was used again in a letter, *Cum inaestimable pretium,* issued by the same Pontiff May 12, 1210, and again in slightly changed form in a letter on the conversion of the Waldensians issued June 14, 1210. The latter letter announced the conversion of one of the leaders of the Waldensian sect and prescribed that the same formula be used when other heretics were received back into the Church.—Cf. Denzinger, n. 420, nota 2.

[24] Cf. Mansi, XXII, 982 et sq.; Denzinger, n. 428-434.

[25] Cf. Schroeder, *Disciplinary Decrees of the General Councils,* p. 237.

The following items represent the decretal law on the subject in Gregory's compilation:

The enactment of Paschal II (1099-1118) contained in a letter to the Archbishop of Palermo that the Apostolic See would not grant the pallium unless he first made a promise of fidelity and obedience to the Holy See. In this promise or oath of fidelity there was contained an oath that the faith which was externally professed by the one making it would be preserved.[26]

In the collection is also included the response of Gregory IX to the Patriarch of Granada in Spain (1227) in which it was stated that a Suffragan Bishop is not bound to take an oath to obey his Metropolitan other than that prescribed by the canons (which also commanded that with the oath there be taken a profession of faith).[27] From the *Registrum* of Gregory III the decretals take the following oath to be made by a Bishop in pledging fidelity to the Pope:

> Ego N. Episcopus ab hac hora in antea fidelis ero Sancto Petro . . . Papatum Romanae ecclesiae et regulas sanctorum patrum adiutor ero ad defendendum et retinendum . . . contra omnes homines . . ." [28]

Finally, the decretals of Gregory contain the instruction of a constitution of Pope Lucius III to a council held in Verona in 1184. It dealt with clerics who had lapsed into heresy and prescribed that they should be deprived of all the prerogatives of their state of life and turned over to the secular arm for punishment unless they retracted their errors publicly before the Bishop and abjured their heresy. Laymen were to be turned over to the secular arm, unless they did likewise.[29]

Though the foregoing items refer only indirectly to the subject

[26] C. 4, X, *de electione,* I, 6; Cf. Mansi, XX, 984;Jaffe, n. 4851. This legislation is taken from *Comp. I,* c. 21, de electione, I, 4. It included the following phrase, ". . . necessitate compellimur iuramentum *pro fide,* pro obedientia, pro unitate requirere. . ." The Glossa suggest that the profession to be sent by Archbishops to Rome be that made by Berengarius before the VI Council of Rome in 1079 (Denzinger, n. 355). Cf. *Decretales D. Gregorii Papae IX suae integritati una cum Glossis Restitutae* (Rome, 1582) p. 111.

[27] C. 13, X, *de maioritate et obedientia,* I, 33; Cf. Potthast, n. 9564.

[28] C. 4 X, *de iureiurando,* II, 24. This is taken from Comp. I, c. 20, *de electione,* I, 4. Practically the same oath is contained in the enactments of the VI Roman Council in 1079. Cf. Mansi, XIX, 900.

[29] C. 9, X, *de hereticis,* V, 7; Jaffe, n. 9635. This law was taken from *Comp.* I, c. 11, *de hereticis,* V, 6.

being treated, they belong at least implicitly to the legislation on the profession of faith already considered, particularly since the oaths of fidelity made by the Bishops, both to the Metropolitans and to the Popes, in addition to assuming the obligation of the profession of faith that had been prescribed for centuries, implied fidelity in orthodoxy as well as in other matters.

There is no direct legislation on the profession of faith contained in the next four decretal collections after the time of Gregory IX—the Liber Sextus of Boniface VIII (1294-1303), the Clementine Constitutions (1311-1312), the Extravagantes of John XII (1316-1334) and the Extravagantes Communes.

Article IV. Summary of Existing Legislation

The considerations advanced in the preceding pages of this work may lead one to the conclusion that by the end of the thirteenth century profession of faith was required of the following:

(1) Those who were to be baptized.

(2) Converts from heresy before they were received into the Church.

(3) Very probably, clerics, before their ordination, if we are to accept the theory that the "examination" required by many of the councils from the time of Nicaea and Laodicea included at least an implicit profession of faith. The oath to keep the faith, imposed by the XI Council of Toledo on all about to be ordained, contained such a profession, at least implicitly.

(4) Bishops, before their consecration, as the evidence of the *Liber Diurnus* shows that this was the practice very probably in use from the fourth or fifth centuries and possibly earlier. In addition to this customary profession, an extraordinary profession of faith was asked for and received by the Pontiffs in the times of heresy and of questioned orthodoxy.

(5) Archbishops before they received the Pallium, as is evidenced by the legislation on the matter by Pope John VIII in the ninth century, and also by a formulary in the *Liber Diurnus* giving a profession for one receiving the pallium.

(6) The Sovereign Pontiffs at the time of their appointments (at least for four centuries, i.e., from the fourth to the eighth, and possibly longer), as is evidenced by the *Liber Diurnus.*

In addition to the profession of faith normally required under ordinary circumstances, extraordinary circumstances frequently imposed the obligation, either by custom or statute, of a special profession of faith. Such was the profession of faith made at the time of heresy and the professions made at the general councils or particular synods. General profession of faith was required of all the faithful when there was danger that heresy would gain ground; confession of the orthodox faith was required of the person suspected of heresy if the demand was made by a superior; particular public profession of faith was required of specific classes of the membership of the Church when they were to obtain new duties, position, or authority.

It remains now to review the canonical effects of neglect of profession of faith normally required of heretics, those to be baptized, the clergy, and the Hierarchy. It is evident that profession of faith was a *sine qua non* condition for admittance into the Church of either non-baptized adults or heretics. Failure to make a profession of faith would bar a person from the reception of this sacrament. There is no evidence of canonical penalty for the members of the clergy who neglected to make the required profession of faith before ordination, save the penalty of deposition for those priests who were ordained without examination and it was later found that they were guilty of some crime at the time of ordination.[30] But this penalty cannot be considered as binding on those who were ordained without examination and were free from crime at that time.

Although the *Liber Diurnus* does not indicate that there was a penalty imposed on those Bishops or Pontiffs who refused to make or neglected to make the profession of faith, the whole tenor of the legislation on profession of faith to be found in that source clearly indicates that neglect of this profession would automatically bar the candidate from the episcopacy or the Papacy. It is, moreover, probable that Archbishops who neglected to make the profession of faith were denied the *pallium,* as Pope John VIII had thus ruled in the case of Willbert and this decision had been included in Gratian's *Decretum.*[31]

[30] Cf. canon 9 of the Council of Nicaea—Mansi, II, 680.
[31] C. 1, D. C.

Article V. The Council of Trent

By far the most articulate and the most important legislation before promulgation of the present Code of Canon Law to deal with the subject of profession of faith was that enacted by the Council of Trent in two of its sessions. It was this council, opened by Paul III in 1545, that confirmed the existing legislation and established substantially the present discipline on the profession of faith.[32]

The reason behind the specific demand for profession of faith by the Council of Trent was, of course, the Reformation, with its attendant evils. Great numbers of the faithful were being led away from the Church; many of the clergy were abandoning the doctrines of Christ for the vagaries of heresy; even those in high places were not immune to the "reform" movement. The Church, realizing the necessity of assuring herself of absolute orthodoxy in her members, re-emphasized, therefore, the necessity of profession of the true faith, especially by those whose duty it was to lead the membership of the Church along the paths of truth.

The first legislation of the Council of Trent regarding profession of faith was prescribed in the instructions on the norm of procedure in the creation of Bishops and Cardinals. In order that the best qualified candidates be elected, the following regulation was adopted:

> That in a provincial synod held by the Metropolitan there shall be prescribed for each place and province a form of examination, scrutiny, or information that shall be the most suitable for those places, so that after the examination or scrutiny of the person who is to be promoted to the Episcopate or the Cardinalate shall have been completed, the form shall, after having been made a public document, be transmitted as soon as possible, together with the attestations thereto and the *profession of faith* of the person to be promoted, to the Sovereign Pontiff in order that he may provide the churches with suitable superiors.[33]

[32] Cf. Augustine, *A Commentary on the New Code of Canon Law* (VI, 3. ed. St. Louis: Herder, 1931), VI, 487; Hinschius, *Das Kirchenrecht der Katholiken und Protestanten in Deutschland,* III, 220; Coronata, *Institutiones Juris Canonici,* II, n. 967, 2; Wernz-Vidal, *Ius Canonicum* (tom. IV, vol. II, *De Rebus, Romae*: Apud Aedes Universitatis Gregorianae, 1936), t. IV, v. II, 21, n. 628.

[33] ". . . mandat sancta synodus, ut in provinciali synodo per metropolitanum habenda, praescribatur quibusque locis et provinciis propria examinis seu inquisitionis aut instructionis faciendae forma, sanctissimi Romani Pontificis arbitrio approbanda, quae magis eisdem locis utilis atque opportuna esse videbitur;

The Council of Trent ruled as follows in the chapter in which were prescribed the qualities of those promoted to dignities and canonries of Cathedral churches and to benefices to which was attached the care of souls:

> Within at least two months of obtaining possession of their offices they shall make a public profession of their orthodox faith before their own Bishop, or, if this latter is hindered from receiving this profession, before his Vicar General or *Officialis.* They shall, moreover, at the same time take an oath that they shall continue in obedience to the Roman Church.
>
> Those promoted to canonries and dignities in Cathedral churches shall be bound, moreover, to make this profession of faith not only before the Bishop or his delegate, but also before the Cathedral chapter.
>
> The penalty for not fulfilling the obligations mentioned above is that the revenues of the canonry or dignity or benefice shall not go to the one who has been promoted to such honors; nor shall the fact of possession be recognized canonically or be of any use to him.[34]

The third important provision on the profession of faith adopted by the Council of Trent was the following:

> Patriarchs, Primates, Archbishops, Bishops, and all others who by right or custom are bound to be present at the provincial council must at the first such synod held [in their territory] after the Council of Trent publicly receive all the

ita tamen, ut, cum deinde hoc examen seu inquisitio de persona promovenda perfecta fuerit, ea in instrumentum publicum redacta cum toto testimonio ac professione fidei ab eo facta quamprimum ad sanctissimum Romanum Pontificem omnino transmittatur, ut ipse summus Pontifex . . . ecclesiis possit utilius providere."—Sess. XXIV *de ref.,* cap. 1. All references and citations of the decrees of Trent are taken from Pelella, *Canones et Decreta Concilii Tridentini ex Editione Romana a MDCCCXXXIV Repetiti* (editio Neapolitana, Neapoli, 1859). The translations of all the decrees of the Council of Trent that are cited in this article are the author's.

[34] "Provisi etiam de beneficiis quibuscunque curam animarum habentibus teneantur a die adeptae possessionis ad minus intra duos menses in manibus ipsius episcopi, orthodoxae suae fidei publicam facere professionem, et in ecclesiae sanctae Romanae obedientia se permansuros spondeant ac iurent.

"Provisi autem de canonicatibus et dignitatibus in ecclesiis cathedralibus non solum coram episcopo seu eius officiali, et etiam in capitulo idem facere teneantur; alioquin praedicti omnes provisi ut supra fructus non faciant suos, nec illis possessio suffragetur."—Sess. XXIV *de ref.,* cap. 12.

things that had been defined and ordained by that holy synod; they must profess obedience to the Sovereign Pontiff and publicly express an anathematization of the heresies that had been condemned by all the canons and the general councils, especially the Council of Trent.

All, moreover, who in the future are promoted to the office of Patriarch, Primate, Archbishop, or Bishop must strictly observe the same legislation regarding the profession of faith, obedience to the Pope, and rejection of heresy at the first provincial synod at which they shall attend.

Should any of the above-mentioned refuse to comply with these ordinances, the Bishops of the same province shall at once inform the Sovereign Pontiff of the refusal and refrain from communion with the recalcitrant individual.

All others who now have benefices or shall hereafter hold them and whose duty it is to be present at the diocesan synod shall do and observe the same as set forth above on the very first occasion that the synod is held. The penalty for the nonobservance of this legislation is punishment according to the norm of the sacred canons.

All those who have charge of universities and general studies, or the visitation or reformation of them shall take care that the canons and decrees of the Council of Trent shall be observed and received, that the masters, teachers, and others in the universities interpret and teach those things which are in conformity to the doctrines of that council, and that at the beginning of each year they bind themselves by solemn oath to this observance.[35]

[35] The entire legislation is as follows: "Praecepit igitur sancta synodus patriarchis, primatibus, archiepiscopis, episcopis, et omnibus aliis qui de iure vel consuetudine in concilio provinciali interesse debent, ut in ipsa prima synodo provinciali, post finem praesentis concilii habenda, ea omnia et singula, quae ab hac synodo definita et statuta sunt, palam recipiant, nec non veram obedientiam summo Romano Pontifici spondeant et profiteantur, simulque haereses omnes a sacris canonibus et generalibus conciliis, praesertimque ab hac eadem synodo damnatas, publice detestentur et anathematizent. Idemque in posterum quicunque in patriarchas, primates, archiepiscopos, episcoposque promovendi in prima synodo provinciali in qua ipsi interfuerint omnino observent. Quod si quis ex supradictis omnibus, quod absit, renuerit, episcopi comprovinciales statim summum Romanum Pontificem admonere sub poena divinae indignationis teneantur, interimque ab eiusdem communione abstineant.

"Ceteri vero omnes sive in praesenti sive in futurum beneficia ecclesiastica habituri, et qui in synodo diocesana convenire debent idem ut supra in ea

A forerunner of the legislation of Pius IV with regard to the profession of faith required of educators in Catholic universities was this regulation concerning the establishment of a chair of Sacred Scripture in public colleges:

> In order that impiety may not be disseminated under the semblance of piety, no one is to be admitted to this chair, whether in public or in private, without having been previously examined and approved of by the Bishop of the place, as to his life, conversation, and knowledge.[36]

Briefly, then, the Council of Trent ruled that the following persons must make a profession of faith:

(1) Those promoted to the dignity of Bishop or Cardinal.

(2) Those promoted to any benefices to which the care of souls was attached, the oath to be taken before the Bishop, or if he was impeded, before the Vicar General or the *Officialis*.

(3) Those promoted to canonries and dignities of Cathedral churches, the oath to be taken before the Bishop or his Vicar General or *Officialis* and also before the Cathedral chapter.

(4) Patriarchs, Primates, Archbishops, Bishops, and all those who by right or custom ought to be present at the provincial council first held in their territory after the Council of Trent.

(5) All those promoted to the dignity of Patriarch, Primate, Archbishop, or Bishop in the future when they attended their first provincial synod.

(6) All others who then held or would hold any ecclesiastical benefice and whose duty it was to be present at the diocesan synod were to make a profession of faith on the

synodo, quae primo quoque tempore celebrabitur, faciant et observent; alias secundum formam sacrorum canonum puniantur.

"Ad haec omnes ii, ad quos universitatum et studiorum generalium cura, visitatio et reformatio pertinet, diligenter curent, ut ab eisdem universitatibus canones et decreta huius sanctae synodi integre recipiantur, ad eorumque normam magistri, doctores, et alii in eisdem universitatibus ea, quae catholicae fidei sunt doceant et interpretentur, seque ad hoc institutum initio cuiuslibet anni solemni iuramento obstringant. . . ."—Sess. XXV *de ref.*, cap. 2.

[36] Sess. V. *de ref.*, cap. 1.

first occasion a diocesan synod would be held after their appointments.

(7) At the beginning of the scholastic year, masters, teachers, and others in universities and colleges of general studies were to take an oath to teach only the orthodox faith.

The penalties established for failure to observe this legislation were as follows:

If those promoted to benefices to which the care of souls was attached, or to canonries and dignities of a Cathedral church did not make their profession of faith within two months of the day they obtained possession, they thereby forfeited the fruits of their office, and they did not enjoy the ordinary rights of possession.

If Primates, Patriarchs, Archbishops, and Bishops, and all those whose duty it was to be present at the provincial synod did not make a profession of faith in the acts and decrees of the Council of Trent at the first provincial synod they attended, they were to be cut off from communion with the other Bishops of the same province and reported to the Holy See.

If holders of any ecclesiastical benefice whose duty it was to be present at the diocesan synod refused or neglected to make a profession of faith at the synod held after this appointment, they were to receive the penalty of the canons, i.e., deprivation of the fruits of their benefice and the right of possession.

Benedict XIV, commenting on this legislation of the Council of Trent, quotes Gavantus to support his opinion that Patriarchs, Primates, Archbishops, and Bishops should not wait until the provincial council to make their profession of faith if there was a diocesan synod held before the particular council.[37]

The same Pontiff held that all who had any ecclesiastical benefice whatsoever were bound to make profession of faith, although the Council of Trent (Sess. XXIV *de ref.*, cap 12) demanded it only of those who were promoted to Cathedral canonries, dignities, and benefices that had attached to them the care of souls. It had been argued from this that those who were promoted to collegiate chapters or to benefices to

[37] Gavantus declares, ". . . laudandi sunt ii episcopi qui in prima sua synodo coram Deo, geneflexi ante altare, fidei professionem emittunt." He then gives as examples of the practice the actions of the Cardinal Archbishops of Naples, Cantelmus and Pignatellus, who made a profession of faith at diocesan synods shortly after the Council of Trent because no provincial synods had been held in their day.—Cf. *De Synodo Dioecesana,* lib. V, cap. II, n. 6.

which was not attached the care of souls were by that token not obliged to make profession of faith. Benedict cites in refutation the rule requiring all who hold any benefice to make profession of faith at the first synod after their appointment.[38]

Regarding the manner in which profession of faith should be made at a synod, the same Pontiff affirmed that it was not necessary that each one recite the formula separately, that it was enough that the secretary of the assembly read it in a clear voice, that all repeat the words after him, and that the members come up by threes or fours to the presiding Bishop, genuflect before him, and with their hands touching the Gospel, recite merely the oath binding them to the profession.[39]

[38] ". . . concludendum est omnes et singulos qui beneficium ecclesiasticum posident in prima synodo dioecesana . . . debere fidei professionem emittere."—*Op. cit.*, lib. V, cap. II, n. 6.

[39] *Op. cit.*, lib. V, cap. II, n. 8.

CHAPTER III

POST-TRIDENTINE LEGISLATION

Article I. The Papal Constitutions

Several important pronouncements were made by Sovereign Pontiffs on the profession of faith within fifty years after the close of the Council of Trent. The first was the constitution of Pope Pius IV (1559-1565), *In sacrosancta,* dated November 13, 1564, which ruled as follows:

No doctor, master, regent, or teacher, either diocesan, regular, or layman, shall assume the position of teaching theology, philosophy, medicine, grammar, or other liberal arts in any university or school in any city, town, or country, even in the places that are in the charge of religious, without first making a profession of faith. Doctors, masters, and scholars shall not proceed to the election of anyone as rector or chancellor of a university or school unless he has made a profession of faith.

No scholar, no matter how worthy of advancement, shall receive any degree unless the doctors, regents, and those professors already appointed to chairs of teaching shall make a profession of faith before the Bishop or his Vicar within three months after the promulgation of this bull, provided they are residents of Italy, or within six months if they live outside of that country. Those promoted to the chairs of teaching in the future must make the profession of faith before the rector or other superiors before their election or appointment. Those to be promoted to the rectorship or chancellorship of a university in the future must make a profession of faith before the Bishop or his Vicar. Scholars to be promoted shall make a profession of faith before the Bishop or his Vicar. Regarding the conferring of the doctorate or other special degrees of this kind, a public document of the profession of faith must be drawn up.

It is forbidden rectors, teachers, and other superiors, and those who have the faculty to teach, no matter what their state of life may be, to retain any chairs of teaching or to try to obtain them, or to receive any degree, unless the provisions mentioned above are fulfilled, under the penalty of interdict for the Bishop who permits it, and excommunication, *lata sententia,* for the others.[1]

The next legislation ordered by Pius IV on profession of faith placed an additional group of beneficiaries under the injunction of the Council of Trent requiring that a profession of faith be taken by all promoted to benefices to which the care of souls was attached, or to Cathedral canonries or dignities, namely, all who were provided with an office of whatever name and title (i. e., religious prelates) by any monastery, convent, or religious house of any order, even military. In order also that there might be uniformity in the profession taken by all, a formula of faith was prescribed to be the official symbol for this act.[2]

The reason for the issuing of the *In sacrosancta* is rather interesting. Pastor in his work on the lives of the Popes affirms that the regulations contained in the bull were occasioned by the complaints of two writers of the day, St. Peter Canisius and Possevino, who had declared that there were rumors to the effect that Protestants were being appointed to posts in Italian universities.[3] Pastor also asserts that it was on the advice of Lainez, General of the Jesuits and close friend of Pius IV, that a demand for profession of faith from aspirants to the doctor's degree was inserted in the legislation.[4]

The regulation of the Council of Trent on the profession of faith to be taken by those who were promoted to the dignity of Bishop[5] was further explained by supplementary provisions of Pope Gregory XIV. This Pontiff ruled that the profession of faith must be made before the prelate who was deputed to make an inquiry in to the faith, life, morals, learning, and prudence of the candidate, or to the

[1] Gasparri, *Codicis Iuris Canonici Fontes* (9 vols., Romae: Typis Polyglottis Vaticanis, 1923-1938), n. 107. Hereafter this work will be cited merely as *Fontes.* The translation of this and the following Papal constitutions is the author's.

[2] "Nos volentes etiam per quoscumque, quibus de monasteriis, conventibus, domibus, et aliis quibuscumque locis regularium quorumque ordinum, etiam militiarum, quocumque nomine, vel titulo providebitur, idem servari, et ad hoc ut unius eiusdem fidei professio uniformiter ab omnibus exhibeatur . . . formam ipsam publicari et observari . . . ac iuxta hanc, et non aliam formam professionem praedictam solemniter fieri, auctoritate Apostolica tenore praesentium districte praecipiendo mandamus huiusmodi sub tenore."—*Iniunctum nobis,* 13 nov. 1564, n. 1—*Fontes,* n. 108.

[3] Pastor, *History of the Popes* (32 vols., St. Louis: Herder, 1906-1940), XVI, 12, nota 1.

[4] *Op. cit.,* p. 93.

[5] Sess. XXIV *de ref.,* cap. 1.

one who had been subdelegated by that prelate to make the inquiry. The prelate, or his subdelegate, the Pope ruled, must receive the profession of faith of the candidate before a notary public and witnesses, and the document of the profession should be signed both by the one making the inquiry and the candidate himself. The sealed and signed document, in authentic form, must then be sent to the Holy See as soon as possible.[6]

Pius V (1556-1572) augmented the legislation of Pius IV by demanding that before they received their degree, doctors of medicine, besides making a profession of faith, must also take an oath before their Ordinary that they would admonish the sick, when called to minister to them, to go to Confession. If the sick person did not respond to this advice within three days, the doctor was to abandon the case.[7]

Benedict XIV in his constitution, *Nuper ad nos,* March 16, 1743, prescribed a profession of faith that was to be taken by the converts of the Maronite sect who wished to enter the true Church.[8]

Amplifying the legislation of Pius IV and Pius V, Leo XII (1823-1829) ruled that aspirants for the baccalaureate or the licentiate must make a profession of faith, using the formula prescribed by Pius IV.[9]

Shortly before the Pontificate of Leo XII, in 1814, when the Pontifical government was restored after the Napoleonic occupation, there arose a controversy about the validity of the degrees granted by the civil government during the time of occupation. In a circular dated June 30, 1814, the Holy See declared that all diplomas issued by the

[6] *Onus Apostolicae,* 15 maii 1591, n. 10—*Fontes,* n. 171.

[7] *Supra Gregem,* 8 martii 1566, n. 6—*Bullarum Diplomatum et Privilegiorum Sanctorum Romanorum Pontificum* (Taurinensis editio, Augustae Taurinorum, 1857-1872), VII, 430. Hereafter this work will be cited as *Bullarium Taurinense.* There is no evidence to show whether the doctors obeyed this prescription for long.

[8] *Bullarium SSmi. Domini nostri Benedicti* XIV (4 vols., 4. ed., Veniciae, 1778), II, 82. Other Papal pronouncements on profession of faith to be taken by those who wished to be reconciled to the Church are to be found in Denzinger, nn. 1083, 1099, 1101, and 1167.

[9] "Qui laurea, aut baccalaureatu aut licentia donatus, is qualibet vice fidei professionem emittat secundum formam a Pio IV praescriptam; medici antequam matriculam accipiant prolibera facultate medicinae exercendae, jurent quemadmodum S. Pius V constituit."—*Quod divina sapientia,* 28 aug. 1824, ad tit. XVII—*Bullarii Romani Continuatio Summorum Pontificum* (19 vols., Prati, 1756-1883), XIII, 107.

civil government granting the doctorate or a professorship by the faculty of the schools of medicine, law, or arts of the Royal (Sapienza) university were null, because they were conferred without a profession of faith by those who received them.[10]

Article II. Responses of the Sacred Congregations

The specific legislation of the Council of Trent and the various Pontiffs did not prevent problems regarding the profession of faith from arising. The solution of the difficulties by the Papal Congregations forms a necessary and interesting portion of the history of the subject. Some of the more important decisions of the Sacred Congregations will be studied forthwith.[11]

Profession of faith according to the formula of Pius IV was so necessary that those who made it according to another form were required to reiterate it before the Bishop at the next diocesan synod.[12] There was no need that a profession of faith be taken by those who had received only simple benefices.[13] Profession of faith demanded from those promoted to dignities or canonries in the Cathedral chapter could not be made by a substitute before the chapter, but must be made by the one who had been elevated to the dignity.[14] Profession of faith before the Vicar General of Rome sufficed for the retaining of the fruits of a benefice, but the profession must be repeated before the beneficiary's Ordinary and the chapter when he returned to his residence.[15] If profession of faith was made before the chapter at which the Vicar General, acting for the Bishop, was present merely as a member of the chapter, and he thus inscribed the profession, omitting the mention of his acting as Vicar General, the profession was nevertheless

[10] *Analecta Iuris Pontificii* (Romae, 1855-1866; Parisiis, 1867-1888), I, 1122. Hereafter this work will be cited by the letters *AIP*.

[11] Cf. Ojetti, *Synopsis Rerum Moralium et Iuris Pontificii* (Romae, 1899), p. 410-411; Barbosa, *Summa Apostolicarum Decisionum* (Lugduni, 1695), p. 564-565.

[12] S.C. Ep. et Reg., *Vercellen.*, 21 iul. 1578—*Fontes*, n. 1335.

[13] S.C.C., *Avenionen.*, mense martii et sept. 1586, § 7—*Fontes*, n. 2155. This ruling has no reference to the profession of faith that had to be taken by *all* beneficiaries who attended a diocesan synod, but only that profession taken upon the reception of a benefice.

[14] S.C.C., *Panormitana*, mense maio 1586; *Valentina*, 5 febr. 1611—*Fontes*, nn. 2167, 2387.

[15] S.C.C., *Bergomen.*, 17 aug. et 25 nov. 1630—*Fontes*, nn. 2524, 2527.

valid.[16] The chapter of canons was obliged to be present to accept the profession of faith. It was not enough that the profession would be made before the member of the chapter who had the greatest dignity or was one of the older canons of the chapter.[17] Illness did not permit a Bishop to appoint a procurator to accept the profession of those who must make it.[18]

Profession of faith was to be made only by the Cathedral canons and not the collegiate canons; the profession was required to be made before the Bishop or his Vicar and also before the chapter. It sufficed that it be made once before the chapter at which the Bishop or his Vicar was present. All who did not comply with these prescriptions were to be deprived of the fruits of their office.[19] It was permitted those who had obtained a benefice to which was attached the care of souls, or dignities, or canonries in the Metropolitan or Cathedral churches to receive the emoluments of office before they had taken possession and made profession of faith;[20] but those who neglected to make a profession of faith within two months also lost the right of prescription.[21]

The custom of making a profession of faith before the chapter alone, especially in those dioceses in which the Ordinary had, besides the Vicar General, a *vicarius de gremio capituli* who convoked the chapter and was the intermediary between the Ordinary and the chapter, was

[16] S.C.C., *Sarzanen.*, 14 ian. 1679, § 1—*Fontes*, n. 2847.

[17] S.C.C., 7 aug. 1683—*Fontes*, n. 2871.

[18] S.C.C., *Calaguritana*, 22 sept. 1696—*Fontes*, n. 2954. The procurator here excluded was not, of course, the substitute recognized by law, the Vicar General or the *Officialis*.

[19] S.C.C., *Cathacen.*, 26 ian., 9 febr. 1726, § 3—*Fontes*, n. 3310.

[20] S.C.C., *Tirasonen.*, 20 apr., 11 maii 1782, § 1—*Fontes*, n. 3821. The reason for this legislation lies in the fact that a period of two months' grace was given for the making of the profession of faith by Sess. XXIV *de ref.*, cap. 12, of the Council of Trent.

[21] S.C.C., *in Tolentina*, 17 apr. 1728—*Thesaurus Resolutionum Sacrae Congregationis Concilii* (Romae, 1718-1908), IV, 174. Hereafter this work will be referred to simply as *Thesaurus*. Cf. also S.C.C., *in Dubium*, 15 dec. 1580, ad cap. 12, Sess. XXIV *de ref.*—Pallottini, *Collectio Omnium Conclusionum et Resolutionum Quae in causis propositis apud Sacram Congregationem Cardinalium S. Concilii Tridentini interpretum Prodierunt ab eius institutione anno MDLXIV ad MDCCCLX, distinctis titulis alphabetico ordine per materias digestas* (18 vols., Romae, 1868-1895), XV, 366, n. 3. Hereafter this work will be referred to as Pallottini. Cf. also S.C.C., *in Nullius*, 1595—Pallottini, XV, 366, n. 4.

abrogated by a decision of the Sacred Congregation of the Council.[22] And in the same response it was decreed that in a revision of the canonries, dignities, and benefices of the Cathedral churches, a profession of faith must be repeated by all.[23] Of considerable importance was the decision that those nominated or deputed by the Order of Jerusalem to benefices to which was attached the care of souls were bound to make a profession of faith before the Archbishop or his consistory before they exercised the care of souls,[24] because the decision set a precedent for future cases in which regulars were involved. The Sacred Congregation also decided that even canons exempt from the jurisdiction of the local Ordinary were bound to make a profession of faith before him;[25] that a beneficiary who was bound to make a profession of faith must fulfill this duty even though no warning of the obligation was given;[26] that those promoted to a benefice or dignity or canonry of the Cathedral church, if they made a profession of faith before they took possession of their new office, were required to make it again within two months under penalty of being deprived of the fruits of their office after the two months had elapsed;[27] that those who had previously made a profession of faith when they accepted a benefice or canonry were obliged to repeat the profession if they received a new benefice or canonry.[28]

The penalties prescribed by the Council of Trent and the various Pontiffs for failure to fulfill the obligation of profession of faith gave

[22] S.C.C., *Hispaniarum,* 1 apr. 1786, § 2—*Fontes,* n. 3851.

[23] *Ibid.,* § 1.

[24] S.C.C., *in Pragen.,* 10 ian. 1798—*Fontes,* nn. 3055, 3059; Pallottini, XV, 366, n. 5.

[25] Pallottini, XV, 366, n. 7.

[26] S.C.C., *in Tolentina*—Pallottini, XV, 366, n. 8.

[27] S.C.C., *in Terasonen.,* 11 maii 1782—*Thesaurus,* LI, 64.

[28] S.C.C., *in Tirasonen.,* 20 apr. 1782—*Thesaurus,* LI, 55. An interesting decision was the following: A Bishop divided two parish churches, and conferred one of them on a new pastor, who thereupon made the required profession of faith. Because of a defect, the giving of the benefice was invalid and a sanation was received from the Holy See. But the new pastor did not make a new profession of faith. Another Bishop, who became Ordinary of the territory in which the above-mentioned parish was located after a division of the diocese, sequestered the fruits of the benefice on the grounds that the pastor, although he had acted in good faith, was not entitled to the fruits of his parish because of a lack of canonical profession of faith. The Sacred Congregation declared that the sequestration should be revoked—S.C.C., *in Ussellen.,* 1 sept. 1759—*Thesaurus,* XXIII, 94.

rise to many controversies as to the exact punishments which were to be meted out to transgressors. The Sacred Congregation of the Council gave the following responses to questions proposed about the penalties:

The daily distributions that accrue to the holders of benefices were not to be considered as part of the fruits, and, therefore, did not cease even though a profession of faith had not been made.[29] Those who did not comply with the obligation of confession of faith, moreover did not lose their vote in the chapter or the right of precedence.[30] Because the clause, "are deprived of the fruits of their office," must be understood also to refer to the fruits of endowments that would come to a beneficiary by reason of his position, the failure to make a profession of faith deprived him of these also.[31]

Because controversy also arose about the obligation of religious to make the profession of faith, several questions were proposed to the Sacred Congregation for solution, which was made as follows:

Regulars obtaining offices or benefices from their own religious order were not bound by the constitution of Pope Pius IV to make a profession of faith;[32] religious who wished to conduct schools, however, could be forced to make a profession by the local Ordinary.[33] Finally, religious who desired to preach in their own churches were not required to make a profession of faith before the local Ordinary, but it could be demanded of them by Bishops before they were allowed to exercise this ministry in those churches not belonging to their institute.[34]

In order to obviate all difficulties of doctors, other professional men, and teachers as to when and if they had to make a profession of faith the Sacred Congregation decided as follows:

Doctors of medicine were to make a profession of faith, or at least to declare that they had made one, when they received their degree;[35] other medical men and lawyers, although they were not bound in all instances to make a profession of faith at the beginning of the exercise

[29] *Pallottini,* XV, 399, n. 9.

[30] *Fontes,* n. 2286; S.C.C., *in Nullius,* 27 apr. 1595—Pallottini, XV, 369, n. 20.

[31] S.C.C., *in Carthaginen.,* 1558—Pallottini, XV, 369, n. 21.

[32] S.C.C., *in Dubia,* 1786—Pallottini, XV, 370, n. 22.

[33] S.C.C., *in Nullius,* 9 apr. 1644—Pallottini, XV, 370, n. 24.

[34] Pallottini, XV, 270, n. 25.

[35] S.C.C., *in Vercellen.*—Pallottini, XV, 370, n. 26.

of their work, were obliged to declare whether or not they had made one when they received their degree; if they had not, they were obliged to make it then.[36] Not only did all doctors and professors of faculties have an obligation to make a profession of faith annually before the Bishop or his Vicar, but also all teachers of arithmetic and similar sciences, even though they did not teach publicly, but did so privately in homes at the expense of private individuals.[37] Public teachers of grammar, arithmetic, music, and other liberal arts, even though they did not conduct schools but taught classes in homes at the expense of others, were similarly bound by the constitution of Pius IV.[38]

The penalties that were prescribed by the constitution of Pius IV for superiors of houses of studies and universities who permitted anyone to teach without a previous examination of faith[39] were also applied by the Sacred Congregation of the Council to Ordinaries who were lax in this regard,[40] by a ruling that the Bishop, if he could possibly do so, must get information about the religious practices and faith of all those who wished to teach any liberal art. He could, therefore, demand a profession of faith from them even though they were teaching in private homes and not in public schools.[41] A custom by which rectors and chancellors of universities omitted profession of faith was condemned by the Sacred Congregation, which also declared that the profession which students took before the superior of studies was approved, even though the latter was not a cleric.[42]

Although those who were appointed to benefices without the care of souls were not bound by the constitution of Pius IV or the Council of Trent to make a profession of faith,[43] custom or diocesan law might legislate in this regard. Such a profession was demanded by synods held in Antwerp (1610), Mechlin (1610), Alexandrina (1732), and under Benedict XIV in Rome.[44]

[36] S.C.C., *in Vercellen.*—Pallottini, XV, 370, n. 27.

[37] S.C.C., *in Ceremonen.*—Pallottini, XV, 370, n. 28.

[38] S.C.C., *in Dubia*—Pallottini, XV, 370, n. 29.

[39] The penalty was excommunication; cf. p. 41.

[40] S.C.C., *in Dubia*—Pallottini, XV, 370, n. 30.

[41] S.C.C., *in Ceremonen.*—Pallottini, XV, 370, n. 31.

[42] S.C.C., *in Urbinaten.*, 10 martii 1633—Pallottini, XV, 370, n. 33.

[43] S.C.C., *in Calaritana.*, 24 ian. 1767—Pallottini, XV, 371, n. 35.

[44] S.C.C., *in Assisien. et Maceraten.*, 21 ian. 1826—*Thesaurus*, LXXXVI, 27; Pallottini, XV, 371, n. 36.

The Sacred Congregation of Indulgences and Sacred Relics was asked whether a new pastor should make a profession of faith the first time he acted in his parish before the congregation and was canonically installed, whether the form of profession should be the same as the form of synodal oath that is found in the *Pontificale Romanum* prescribed for a synod, and should it be recited in the vernacular.

The response was that the decree of Sess. XXIV *de ref.* of the Council of Trent must be observed, and the profession must be that prescribed by Pius IV.[45] The Council of Trent, it must be remembered, allowed two months' grace for the profession of faith after a benefice had been acquired. This response, therefore, did not change that ruling.

A Vicar Apostolic in China explained that he did not make the profession of faith required by Pius IV before his consecration, believing that the oath contained in the *Pontificale Romanum* and the profession were one and the same. He, therefore, asked for absolution from the Holy See from any censure he may have incurred.

The absolution was granted, in so far as it was needed, by Pope Pius IX, who also reaffirmed the obligation of Vicars Apostolic to make the profession of faith prescribed by Pius IV.[46] The Sacred Congregation of the Propagation of the Faith declared that the custom of Bishops to make a profession of faith in provincial synods, even though they had already made the canonical profession, was praiseworthy.[47] It was decided, too, that those who did not make a profession of faith within the required time would be obliged to apply to the Holy See both for the faculty of validly making the profession and for the condonation of the receiving of the fruits of their benefice.[48]

Article III. Legislation of Particular Councils After Trent

The instructions of the Council of Trent and the pronouncements of the several Pontiffs on profession of faith after that council constituted universal law. They did not, however, obstruct the progress of particular law on the subject. Thus, it is found that the subsequent particular councils or synods almost universally reaffirmed the doctrine

[45] S.R.C., *Briocen.*, 21 iul. 1855, n. 9—*Fontes*, n. 5976.

[46] S.C. de Prop. Fide., 10 ian. 1875—*Fontes*, n. 4886.

[47] S.C. de Prop. Fide. (C.G.), 26 febr. 1875—*Fontes*, n. 4887.

[48] S.C.C., *in Civitaten.*, 2 sept. 1599—*Fontes*, n. 2328.

of the Council of Trent and of Pius IV on profession of faith, and in some instances extended the obligation to persons not mentioned in the Tridentine or Papal legislation.

At the I Provincial Council of Milan in 1565, all the provisions of the Council of Trent and of Pius IV were repeated, with the warning that Bishops must see to it that those who had been promoted to benefices to which was attached the care of souls, and those who had received the doctorate, would make a profession of faith within a month; and that the profession would also be made by those who in any manner taught children or adolescents in any of the arts, even in the rudiments of grammar.[49] The III Provincial Council of Milan (1573) extended the obligation of profession of faith to all teachers;[50] the IV Provincial Council of Milan specifically mentioned that teachers of arithmetic, all liberal arts, and music were included in the legislation on the profession of faith,[51] and the provisions of the V Provincial Council of Milan ruled that no one, not even regulars in their own churches, should be permitted to preach unless they had made a profession of faith before the Bishop or his Vicar. Once they had made it, however, they were not obliged to repeat it before the same Bishop for the same cause. Confessors, religious as well as seculars, were bound by the same regulation.[52] The same council also prescribed that a profession of faith would need to be made by all physicians and surgeons within three months. It further ordered that in the future no physician or surgeon should be allowed to begin practice unless he made the required profession. The same was ordered for all advocates and procurators of the Sacred Inquisition.[53]

The ruling of a council held in Narbonne in 1609 is significant, for it gives an indication of the mind of the French Church authorities in this matter. It follows:

> . . . mandavimus ut omnes qui ad quaecumque aut qualiacumque officia onera, et beneficia ecclesiastica, regularia et secularia, cum vel sine cura, in posterum promovebuntur, priusquam fructus eorumdem faciant suos, professio fidei . . . illis suffragentur in manibus ordinariorum beneficii sibi collati sive saeculares sint aut regulares emittant. Quod si absentibus

[49] Cf. Hardouin, X, 637 C, D, E; Mansi, XXIV a, 5.

[50] Cf. Hardouin, X, 769.

[51] Cf. Hardouin, X, 806; Mansi, XXXIV a, 182 D.

[52] Cf. Hardouin, X, 954.

[53] *Loc. cit.*

> fiat collatio tenebitur provisus, coram Ordinario loci in quo residet eamdem fidei professionem emittere. . . Eamdem profitebuntur scholarum magistri et qui ad sacros ordines promovebuntur aut doctoratus alteriusve gradus insignia recipient; quod idem praestabunt curati omnes, et alii de jure vel consuetudine in synodis dioecesanis et in conciliis provincialibus assistentes priusquam ad alia progrediantur.[54]

The decrees of a provincial synod held in Rouen in this period (within forty years of the Council of Trent) ruled that profession of faith must be made by all promoted to sacred orders; to any type of ecclesiastical office, benefice, or duty;[55] and that every year the profession must be repeated in the episcopal synods by those who had benefices to which was attached the care of souls, as well as by vicars, and, in their yearly chapters, by all canons, chaplains, and religious.[56]

The promulgation of the provisions of the Council of Trent and of Pius IV was speedily observed in Belgium. In 1570 the Provincial Council of Mechlin observed: "ut omnia et singulis . . . quae in sacro concilio tridentino decreta et statuta sunt inviolabitur observentur. . ."[57] Even earlier the Council of Cambrai of 1565 in a decree, entitled "De Libris Haereticorum, Suspectis, et Vetitis," demanded that the Bishops act with the civil authorities in enforcing the order of the Emperor Charles V that printers and booksellers make a profession of faith.[58] This regulation was intended to safeguard the people against the spread of heretical works, especially those condemned in the *Roman Index of Forbidden Books*. It was because of such precautions that Belgium remained, to a great extent, a Catholic nation. Some of the credit for the prevention of the spread of heresy must also go to the civil government, as is evidenced in the following incident:

The Spanish governor of the Belgian provinces issued an edict approving the decrees of this council. By royal decree he ordered all

[54] Cf. Hardouin, XI, 4 E, 5 AB.

[55] "Inter ipsos tamen volumus comprehendi scholarum, fabricarum, hospitalium, fraternitatum, et quarumque communitatum piarum, magistros, rectores, sodales, et administratores."—Hardouin, X, 1213, 1214.

[56] *Loc. cit.*

[57] Cf. Mansi, XXXIV a, 579.

[58] "Rogentur quoque iidem magistratus ut in singulos annos fidem ex formula Concilii Tridentini profiteantur iidem typographi ac librarii. . . ." *AIP* VI, 1728. Hartzheim, *Concilia Germania* (11 vols., Coloniae Augustae Agrippinensium, 1759-1790), VII, 98. Hereafter this work will be cited by the use of the author's name.

magistrates, booksellers, printers, schoolmasters and schoolmistresses, without exception, to make an annual profession of faith according to an abridged formula of Pius IV. He also demanded that masters of Latin schools make the profession according to the complete formula of the above-mentioned Pontiff. The edict also ordered that all civil magistrates in the districts, all public officers, bailiffs, provosts, councilors, pensioners, and court attaches would be obliged to make a profession of faith, at the same time touching a crucifix or a book of the Gospels. In the formula for the civil magistrates was contained the clause that the person taking it swore before God that he believed all that the Roman Catholic Church taught, that he was submissive to the Pope, and that he detested the doctrines of the Lutherans, the Calvinists, the Anabaptists, and other heresies and sects.[59]

Another council held in Cambrai in 1586 stressed the obligation of profession of faith for "all professors, preachers, confessors, schoolmasters, and, moreover, printers, publishers, and all who distribute books, both men and women."[60] The same council also demanded that those who had once lapsed into heresy and then returned to the Church would be required to give ample proof of their conversion by means of testimonial letters of the pastor of their last parish, if they were traveling from place to place, before they were admitted to the sacraments. This testimony could be given by a pastor only if the converted heretics had professed the true faith to him, or, to the pastor's knowledge, to some other priest.[61] This council also asked that the government assure itself of the faith of all civil magistrates by demanding of them a profession of Catholic faith before they were admitted to office.[62]

The provisions of Cambrai were repeated in the Synods of Tournai in 1589 and 1600,[63] Namur in 1604,[64] Mechlin in 1607,[65] and Ant-

[59] Cf. Hartzheim, VII, 1932; *AIP,* 1733-1734.

[60] The reason given was this: "Cum fides sit verum symbolum quo catholici ab aliis discernuntur, sine qua impossibile est placere Deo."—Hartzheim, VII, 997, 998; *AIP,* VI, 1733; Mansi, XXXIV b, 1227-1228.

[61] Cf. Hartzheim, VII, 997, 998; *AIP,* VI, 1733; Mansi, XXXIV b, 1227, 1228.

[62] Cf. Hartzheim, VII, 997, 998; *AIP,* VI, 1733; Mansi XXXIV b, 1227, 1228.

[63] Cf. Hartzheim, VII, 1038-1039; *AIP,* VI, 1734.

[64] Cf. Hartzheim, VII, 608; *AIP,* VI, 1735.

[65] Cf. Hartzheim, VIII, 774-775;*AIP,* VI, 1736-1737; Mansi, XXXIV b, 1443.

werp in 1610. The last named synod seems to have been the first that actually designated the Bishop or the Vicar General as the one to whom the profession of faith was to be made by all who in any way were connected with the distribution of books. It also settled the date, January 2 of each year, on which the profession was to be made.[66]

The Tridentine provisions regarding the profession of faith were re-emphasized at councils held at Metz in 1610,[67] at Rouen in 1618,[68] at Rheims in 1583,[69] at Tours in 1583,[70] and at Borgo San Sepolcro in Italy in 1584.[71]

A study of the conciliar decrees of the late sixteenth and early seventeenth centuries in Belgium shows that the provincial synods greatly influenced those held in the various dioceses of the province, and even the decrees of nearby provinces in Belgium. Because of this fact the legislation on profession of faith passed by the Provincial Council of Mechlin in 1607 was repeated by the synods of Bois-le Duc in 1612,[72] Gand in 1613,[73] Cambrai in 1631,[74] and Namur-Antwerp in 1639.[75]

One may conclude, therefore, that at this particular period there existed in Belgium a constant realization that profession of faith was a requisite for the safeguarding of faith, that it was one of the most potent means of combating the pernicious errors of the pseudo-reformers, who used the newly discovered process of printing as a novel means of spreading and propagating their false doctrine.

The Church in other lands also realized the necessity of the making of a profession of faith by those who were by office destined to lead the people in spiritual matters, especially Bishops and pastors. This can be seen from a study of the decrees of the Provincial Councils of Mexico City in 1585,[76] Aquila in Italy in 1596,[77] Naples in 1596,[78]

[66] Cf. Hartzheim, VIII, 986; *AIP,* VI, 1739.
[67] Cf. Hartzheim, VIII, 950.
[68] Cf. Mansi, XXXIV a, 618.
[69] Cf. Mansi, XXXIV a, 684.
[70] Cf. Mansi, XXXIV a, 807.
[71] Cf. Mansi, XXXIV a, 875.
[72] Cf. Hartzheim, IX, 202-204.
[73] Cf. Hartzheim, IX, 242-243.
[74] Cf. Hartzheim, IX, 538-540.
[75] Cf. Hartzheim, IX, 572; also *AIP,* VI, 1740-1745.
[76] Cf. Mansi, XXXIV b, 1022.
[77] Cf. Mansi, XXXIV b, 1367.
[78] Cf. Mansi, XXXV b, 809.

Salermo in 1696,[79] and Besancon in 1571.[80] At a provincial council held in Naples in 1699 the regulations of the Council of Trent and Pius IV were promulgated and the obligation of profession of faith was extended to preachers, religious as well as secular, and to those who aspired to the doctorate or any degree.[81]

The crystallization of the entire legislation in the matter of the profession of faith is to be found in the decrees of a council held at Rome in the reign of Benedict XIV, in 1725, in which it was declared that the following were required to make a profession of faith:

(1) Bishops and other members of the clergy recently promoted to ecclesiastical benefices or about to be initiated into sacred orders.

(2) Those who obtained canonries or dignities.

(3) Those promoted to benefices to which was attached the care of souls.

(4) Those promoted to simple benefices.

(5) Vicars General, Vicars Forane, procurators and promotors of the Episcopal revenues, the Chancellor, and other officers of the Curia.

(6) New preachers, even regulars.

(7) New confessors, even those of nuns.

(8) Public and private teachers of theology, philosophy, canon law, civil law, and of elementary studies, even in primary schools.

(9) Those exercising the practice of surgery or medicine.[82]

Historical Summary and Conclusions

Profession of faith was considered necessary even in the very infancy of the Church. As early as the fourth century there existed

[79] Cf. Mansi, XXXV b, 967, 968.

[80] Cf. Mansi, XXVI Bis, 38-39.

[81] Cf. *Acta et Decreta Sacrorum Conciliorum Recentiorum Collectio Lacensis* (7 vols., Friburgi Brisgoviae, 1870-1890), I, 158, 159. Hereafter this work will be cited by the words *Collectio Lacensis.*

[82] Cf. *Collectio Lacensis,* I, 345-346; S.C.C., *in Comacelen,* 24 aug. 1822—Pallottini, XV, 371-372, n. 37.

legislation regarding the formalities of profession of faith for those about to be baptized and for converts to the Church. The demand that a profession of faith be made by Bishops, particularly the Pope, very probably dates back also to the fourth century, as is evidenced by the formularies contained in the *Liber Diurnus*. The practice of demanding a profession of faith from those about to be ordained certainly goes back to the ninth century and is probably much older, although there is no conclusive evidence for its existence before that time.

The present legislation on the profession of faith was crystallized in the decrees of the Council of Trent and the constitutions of several of the Roman Pontiffs who spoke on the subject after that council, notably of Pope Pius IV. The application of the decrees of the Council and the Pontiffs has been explained in the decisions of the Papal Congregations for several centuries.

PART TWO
CANONICAL COMMENTARY

CHAPTER IV

THE PERSONAL OBLIGATION OF PROFESSION OF FAITH

Canon 1407.—Obligationi fidei professionem emittendi non satisfacit qui eam per procuratorem vel coram laico emittit.

The personal obligation of making a profession of faith has been recognized since the first legislation on the subject. It has been shown in preceding chapters [1] that in response to questions the Holy See has always demanded that the one obligated to a profession of faith should fulfill this duty himself. There has been considerable controversy on the matter, however, and at one time the validity of profession of faith made by a proxy was upheld by canonists of great repute.[2] Reiffenstuel, one of these, quoted the opinion of Barbosa, Sanchez, Tamburinus, and others in support of his assertion that the profession could be made by proxy. His argument in brief was this: What one can do himself, he can do through another, provided there is no prohibition of law that hinders such action. Neither the Council of Trent nor the bull of Pope Pius IV prohibited the making of a profession of faith by proxy. He concluded, therefore, that a proxy could validly be employed.[3] Why he should have held this opinion in view of the very definite contrary decisions of the Holy See [4] is difficult to determine. Be that as it may, however, the pre-Code decisions of the Sacred Congregation of the Council on this question are vindicated by the present discipline,[5] which is so strict that not even

[1] Cf. *supra*, p. 43.

[2] Cf. Augustine, *A Commentary,* VI, 490.

[3] Cf. *Ius Canonicum Universum* (5 vols. in 7, Parisiis, 1894), I, 94.

[4] S.C.C., *Panormitana,* mense maio 1586—*Fontes,* n. 2167; *Valentina,* 5 febr. 1611—*Fontes,* n. 2387.

[5] Cf. Coronata, *Institutiones,* II, 351; Vermeersch—Creusen, *Epitome Iuris Canonici* (3 vols., I, 6. ed., 1937; II, III, 5. ed., 1936, Mechliniae-Romae: H. Dessain), II, 519; Beste, *Introductio in Codicem* (Collegeville, Minn.: St. John's Abbey Press, 1938), p. 694; De Meester, *Iuris Canonici et iuris Canonico-Civilis Compendium* (3 vols. in 4, nova editio, Brugis: Desclee, De Brouwer & Si., 1923), III, 317; Prümmer, *Manuale Iuris Canonici* (3. ed., Friburgi Brisgoviae: Herder & Co., 1922), p. 492.

the Ordinary could permit one bound to a profession of faith to make it by proxy.[6] It must be remembered, moreover, that while the obligation of making a profession of faith devolves personally on all those mentioned in canon 1406, superiors are indirectly bound to see to it that their subjects make the required profession.[7]

The present law also demands that the profession of faith be made before a cleric. The obligation cannot be satisfied, therefore, by a profession of faith made before a layman. The reason for this lies in the fact that the latter lacks spiritual and juridical power to receive a profession of faith, itself a juridical act.[8]

A. *The Formula to Be Used*

The historical portion of this work has discussed how at various periods in the existence of the Church various formulas were used by those persons bound by law to make a profession of faith. As the exigencies of the time demanded or as Pope or council decided, the formulas were changed to meet the specific attacks of heretics or to emphasize some doctrinal teaching of the Church.[9] Under the present legislation those bound to make a profession of faith by reason of canon 1406 must use the formula that is found at the beginning of the Code.[10] This formula, which is substantially that introduced by Pope Pius IV in his constitution, *Iniunctum nobis,* December 13, 1564,[11] was modified by the additions decreed by the Sacred Congregation of the Council on January 20, 1877, after the Council of the Vatican.[12]

It is not to be confused with those professions of faith in use by reason of the prescriptions of liturgical laws, viz., the formula of

[6] Cf. Blat, *Commentarium Textus Codicis Iuris Canonici* (5 vols. in 7, Romae: Collegio "Angelico," 1921-1938; III, *De Rebus,* 2. ed., 1934), III, 428.

[7] Cf. Aertnys-Damen, *Theologia Moralis* (2 vols., 11. ed., Taurinorum Augustae: Marietti, 1928), I, 218; De Meester, *Compendium,* III, 317; Vermeersch-Creusen, *Epitome,* II, 739; Coronata, *Institutiones,* II, 351.

[8] Cf. Augustine, *A Commentary,* VI, 490; Blat, *op. cit.,* 428; De Meester, *loc. cit.*

[9] Cf. Coronata, *Institutiones,* II, 349.

[10] This is repeated in Appendix I of the Code.

[11] Cf. *Fontes,* n. 108.

[12] Cf. *ASS,* X (1877), 74; Aertnys-Damen, *Theologia Moralis,* I, 217, in nota 3; Coronata, *op. cit.,* 349, in nota 1.

profession of faith taken by those about to be baptized,[13] the formula used by heretics returning to the faith,[14] and the formula used at the time of the ordination of priests.[15] These lie outside the field of the subject matter being treated and are governed by the existing liturgical laws, which have their own binding force.[16]

[13] Cf. *Rituale Romanum* (editio Vaticana, Taurini-Romae: Marietti, 1926), tit. 2, c. 4, n. 32.

[14] Cf. C.S.C. Off., 20 iulli 1859; *Collectanea C. Congregationis de Propaganda Fidei* (2 vols., Romae, 1907), n. 1178. A new formula was approved recently by the Sacred Congregation of the Holy Office. Cf. *Homiletic and Pastoral Review* XLII (1942), 772-773.

[15] Cf. *Pontificale Romanum* (Ratisbonae, 1891), "De Ordinatione Presbyteris."

[16] Canon 2. ". . . Quare omnes liturgicae leges vim suam retinet, nisi earum aliqua in Codice expresse corrigatur." Cf. Aertnys- Damen, *op. cit.*, 218-219.

CHAPTER V

PERSONS REQUIRED BY THE CODE TO MAKE PROFESSION OF FAITH

The Council of Trent established substantially the present discipline on the profession of faith and later pre-Code decrees merely specified more accurately the persons who were bound.[1] The present legislation, therefore, is to be interpreted in accordance with the commentary of the approved authors on the old law, in so far as the Code law is merely a re-statement of the old discipline.[2] Since in some instances, however, there has been a modification in the legislation on profession of faith, the interpretation according to the commentary of approved pre-Code authors must be restricted to those parts which agree with the old law and the meaning of the words of the present law must govern in those parts which contain the modification.[3]

In the following articles the persons who are bound by the Code to make a profession of faith are considered separately.

ARTICLE *I.* THOSE WHO ATTEND COUNCILS OR SYNODS

Canon 1406.—§ 1. Obligatione emittendi professionem fidei, secundum formulam a Sede Apostolica probatam, tenentur:

1°. Coram praeside eiusve delegato, qui Oecumenico vel particulari Concilio aut Synodo dioecesanae intersunt cum voto seu consultivo seu deliberativo; praeses autem coram eodem Concilio vel Synodo;

Prior to the Council of Trent there was no general legislation requiring a profession of faith from those who attended either Ecumenical or Particular Councils, although it was a custom universally followed that all those who had a vote at such councils should make a profession of faith. It has been indicated in earlier portions of this work that one of the first acts of practically every council was the profession of

[1] Cf. Augustine, *A Commentary,* VI, 487; Ayrinhac, *Administrative Legislation in the New Code of Canon Law* (New York: Longmans, Green & Co., 1930), p. 303; Blat, *Commentarium,* III, 422.

[2] Cf. Canon 6, 2°.

[3] Cf. Canon 6, 3°.

faith by the members attending.[4] The Council of Trent was specific in demanding that all Bishops and all beneficiaries who attended either particular council or diocesan synod should there make a profession of faith.[5] The present law goes further in demanding a profession of faith from all who have either a decisive or consultive vote in Ecumenical, Plenary, or Particular Council and Diocesan Synod. In the following each type of council or synod is considered separately.

A. *Ecumenical Councils*

According to the legislation of the Code only the Roman Pontiff can validly convoke an Ecumenical Council, and only either he or his delegate can validly preside, determine the matters to be discussed, and confirm the decrees that are adopted.[6] The law requires that the following persons are called to an Ecumenical Council. By reason of their having a decisive vote they are bound to make profession of faith.

1. The Cardinals of the Holy Roman Church, even though they may not be Bishops.
2. Patriarchs, Primates, Archbishops, and residential Bishops, even those not yet consecrated.
3. Abbots and Prelates *nullius.*
4. The Abbot Primate, abbots who are superiors of monastic congregations, and the supreme heads of exempt organizations of the religious clergy.[7]

The Code likewise provides that if Titular Bishops are called, they have a decisive vote, unless it is otherwise stated in the decree of convocation.[8] Besides the persons enumerated above no one is endowed either by divine or ecclesiastical right with a decisive vote at an Ecumenical Council, unless by extraordinary Apostolic indult

[4] Cf. p. 10.

[5] Cf. Sess. XXV *de ref.*, cap. 2.

[6] Canon 222; cf. Vermeersch-Creusen, *Epitome,* I, 283; Coronata, *Institutiones,* I, 384; Wernz-Vidal, *Ius Canonicum* (II, *De Personis,* ed. altera, Romae: Apud Aedes Universitatis Gregorianae, 1928), II, 447-450.

[7] Canon 223, § 1, 1°, 2°, 3°, 4°. Cf. Coronata, *Institutiones, loc. cit.;* Wernz-Vidal, *Ius Canonicum,* II, 451.

[8] Canon 223, § 2. Cf. Wernz-Vidal, *Ius Canonicum,* II, 450, 451.

the procurator of an absent Bishop, a diocesan administrator, or a vicar capitular were given such a vote.[9] If these conditions are verified, however, both the latter two classes enumerated above must make a profession of faith.

The Code also decrees that theologians and experts in canon law may be called to a council, but it provides that they have merely a consultive vote.[10] It also provides that the superiors of non-exempt clerical religious congregations are not to be called to an Ecumenical Council, unless the bull of convocations expressly states otherwise. But even in the event they were called, they would have no vote, either decisive or consultive.[11] It must be remembered, however, that if the decree of convocation gave such superiors a consultive vote they, together with the theologians and experts in canon law who might have been called to the council, must make a profession of faith, for the obligation of the profession bids those with *consultive* as well as decisive vote.

Ordinarily proxies of the persons who, though called to an Ecumenical Council are impeded from attending, are allowed to be present only at the public sessions of the council and have no vote, either decisive or consultive.[12] They have no obligation, therefore, because of this lack of franchise, to make a profession of faith at any time during the sessions of the council.

B. *Plenary Councils*

With the permission of the Holy See the Ordinaries of several ecclesiastical provinces may meet in plenary council, which is convoked by a legate appointed by the Holy See. The legate also presides

[9] Cf. Wernz-Vidal, *op. cit.*, 452. It is unlikely that such an indult would be given. At the Vatican Council the proxies of absent Bishops were without vote and had the right merely of signing the acts of the council and of attending the solemn sessions of the meeting. Cf. Benedict XIV, *De Synodo Dioecesana,* I, III, c. 12, n. 5.

[10] Canon 223, § 3. Cf. Wernz-Vidal, *op. cit.*, 452. These are not to be confused with the theologians and canon law experts who might assist the fathers of the council in a private manner. Cf. Coronata, *Institutiones.* I, 385, nota 4.

[11] Cf. canon 223, § 1, 4°. Such superiors were not called to the Vatican Council. Cf. Wernz-Vidal, *op. cit.* 451.

[12] Canon 224, § 2. They may, however, subscribe the acts of the council. Cf. Coronata, *Institutiones,* I, 385.

over the sessions.[13] The following have to make a profession of faith at a plenary council by reason of the decisive vote they exercise:

The Papal Legate, the Archbishops, the residential Bishops (who may send their Coadjutors or Auxiliary Bishops to take their place and cast their votes as proxies), the Apostolic Administrators of dioceses, Abbots and Prelates *nullius,* Vicars and Prefects Apostolic, and Vicars Capitular.[14] If Titular Bishops who reside in the territory where the council is held are also summoned to the council by the Papal Legate, they also have an obligation to make a profession of faith, as they have a decisive vote, unless the contrary is expressly stated.[15]

Other members of the secular or religious clergy who are invited to attend the plenary council also have an obligation to make profession of faith, for they have a consultive vote.[16]

C. *Provincial Councils*

At the provincial councils to be held every twenty years by the prescription of the Code[17] the following have a decisive vote: The Metropolitan who calls the council and the Suffragan Bishops of the province, together with the Vicars and Prefects Apostolic and Vicars Capitular. To this list must be added Archbishops, Bishops, and Abbots and Prelates *nullius* who have, with the approval of the Holy See, attached themselves to a neighboring Metropolitan, because, in the case of the Archbishop, he has no Suffragan Bishops, and, in the case of the others, they are not suffragan to any Metropolitan.[18] All of those listed above must make a profession of faith by virtue of canon 1406, § 1, 1°. If the Titular Bishops who reside in a province are called to the council by the one who presides, with the consent of the majority of those who have a decisive vote, they have a decisive vote, unless the majority of those who have by law a decisive vote

[13] Canon 281. Cf. Coronata, *Institutiones,* I, 438; Vermeersch-Creusen, *Epitome,* I, 312.

[14] Canon 282, § 1.

[15] Canon 282, § 3.

[16] Canon 282, § 3.

[17] Canon 283. Cf. Wernz-Vidal, *Ius Canonicum,* II, 566-580.

[18] Canon 286, § 1.

expressly provide the contrary in the document of convocation.[19] If they are given a decisive vote in the proceedings of the council, they must make a profession of faith with the others.

By reason of having a consultive vote the following who attend a provincial council must also make a profession of faith: The two members of the Cathedral chapter or diocesan consultors who have been voted to represent their respective groups after an invitation to attend has been issued to them, as required by law; the major superiors of exempt clerical religious congregations and the superiors of the monastic congregations who live within the province and who, as required by law, have been invited to attend the council; and, finally, those members of the secular or religious clergy who may be summoned to the council.[20] The proxies of those with decisive votes who have been impeded from attending a provincial council have merely a consultive vote, unless they have a decisive vote from another title (e.g., if one Suffragan acted as proxy for another, in which case, however, he is forbidden to cast a double vote).[21] These proxies, nevertheless, in virtue of that consultive vote, are under obligation to make the profession of faith at the proper time. It should be noted, moreover, that the Code gives a consultive vote only to those members of the religious or secular clergy who have been invited or summoned to attend the council. If priests are present at the sessions without any official invitation, they are not obliged to make a profession of faith.[22]

D. *Diocesan Synods*

The following, by reason of having a consultive vote, are bound to a profession of faith at a diocesan synod, the convocation of which is reserved by law to the Bishop:

1. The Vicar General.
2. The canons of the Cathedral church or the diocesan consultors.
3. The rector of the diocesan seminary, at least the rector of the major seminary.

[19] Canon 286, § 2.

[20] Canon 286, §§ 3, 4.

[21] Canon 287, § 2.

[22] Cf. Augustine, *A Commentary* (II, 6. ed., St. Louis: Herder, 1936), II, 302, 303; Coronata, *Institutiones,* I, 442, 443; Vermeersch-Creusen, *Epitome,* 1, 313, 314.

4. The vicars forane.
5. One deputy from each collegiate church who has been chosen by the members of the collegiate chapter.
6. At least one pastor from each deanery who has been chosen by the priests of the deanery who have the care of souls.
7. The pastors of the city where the synod is held.
8. Abbots who are actual superiors of abbeys and one of the superiors of each clerical religious organization in the diocese, to be designated by the provincial, unless the latter resides in the diocese, in which case he himself may go to the synod.
9. All the canons, pastors, religious superiors, or any or all of the secular priests of the diocese whom the Bishop invites to the synod. These latter have a right to vote unless the Bishop in the invitation states otherwise.[23]

Here again it must be remembered that all clerics who are present as mere onlookers, or those clerics who are indeed present by invitation, but are without vote, are not bound to make a profession of faith with the others.

The Code allows those who attend a council or a synod with either a decisive or a consultive vote to make their profession either before the presiding officer or his delegate, who may be any priest, but who should be one endowed with some ecclesiastical dignity or with some special prerogative of position or seniority.[24] It is not necessary that all who are bound to make the profession do so individually. One may read the formula, the others repeating it phrase for phrase after him, or one may read the entire formula or profession orally and the others give their assent to it at the end in a few words, taking the oath individually with one hand on a book of the Gospels.[25]

[23] Canon 358, § 1. The Bishop has the only decisive vote in a diocesan synod.

[24] Cf. S. C. Consist., 25 oct. 1910, ad VIII—*AAS,* II, 857; "Ad fidei professionem recipiendum delegari potest quilibet clericus, decet autem ut sacerdos delegetur et pro emittentis dignitate, sacerdos in dignitate constitutus . . . "—Coronata, *Institutiones,* II, 349.

[25] Cf. S. C. Consist., 25 oct. 1910, ad IV—*AAS,* II, 856; Ayrinhac, *Administrative Legislation,* pp. 305, 306; Coronata, *Institutiones,* II, 351; Wernz, *Ius Decretalium,* III, n. 19; Benedict XIV (*De Synodo Dioecesana,* I, V, cap. 2, n. 8) says that it is enough that the secretary of the synod read the profession

While it is not the intention of this work to describe the ceremony of synodal profession of faith, it may be indicated that in provincial councils and diocesan synods the profession takes place immediately after the reading of the preliminary decrees in the first session. The presiding Bishop or Metropolitan first makes the profession and then it is taken by those bound by law.[26]

Article II. Those Who Preside at Councils and Synods

The Code is explicit in demanding that those who preside over a council or a synod must themselves make a profession of faith before the assembled fathers. As has been indicated above, the Pope or his legate presides at an Ecumenical council; a legate appointed by the Holy See is the presiding officer of a plenary council; the Metropolitan of a province or (if the Metropolitan see is vacant or the incumbent is impeded from calling a council) the senior Suffragan presides at a provincial council, and the Bishop or Vicar General, if the latter has a special mandate, presides at a diocesan synod.[27]

As has been indicated earlier in this work, the Council of Trent legislated concerning the profession of faith that must be taken at councils and synods. It ruled that all those promoted to the office of Patriarch, Primate, Archbishop, or Bishop must make a profession of faith at the first provincial synod at which they were in attendance.[28] Benedict XIV, commenting on this legislation of the Council of Trent, was of the opinion that all those mentioned above should not wait until a provincial council was held, but should make their profession of faith at a diocesan synod, if it was held before the provincial council.[29] That the prescriptions of the Council of Trent on the matter were followed until the advent of the Code of Canon Law in 1918 there can be no doubt.[30] But in some instances only the letter of the law

of faith in a loud voice and that all repeat the words after him. At the end all approach the presiding Bishop by threes or fours, genuflect before him, and, with their hands touching the book of the Gospels, say singly: "Ego N. N. spondeo, voveo, ac juro; sic me Deus, etc."

[26] Cf. Messmer, *Praxis Synodalis* (2. ed., New York, 1886), pp. 53, 54; Bendecit XIV, *loc cit.*

[27] Cf. Canons 222, 281, 284, and 357.

[28] Sess. XXV *de ref.*, cap. 2.

[29] *De Synodo Dioecesana,* lib. V, cap. II, n. 6.

[30] Cf. Wernz, *Ius Decretalium,* III, n. 15; Coronata, *Institutiones,* II, 350; Guilday in his *A History of the Councils of Baltimore* (New York: The

was followed and profession of faith was made only by those Bishops who were attending a council for the first time since their consecration. This is evidenced in a response of the Sacred Congregation of the Propagation of the Faith to the Archbishop of Westminster in England in 1860. Mildly reproving the prelate for permitting the synod previously held in Westminster to demand profession of faith only from those Bishops attending for the first time, the Sacred Congregation affirmed that it was a universal practice for all the assembled fathers in council to make a profession of faith.[31]

The question arises: Does the above-quoted legislation of the Council of Trent hold? Are the Bishops who attend the first council or synod after their consecration to make a profession of faith in addition to that they must make as members of the council with decisive or consultive vote?

There can be no doubt that this legislation is now abrogated. Canon 6, 6°, declares that all disciplinary laws that were in force before the Code and are not explicitly or implicitly contained in the Code have lost their force.[32] The provision that newly consecrated Bishops, Patriarchs, Primates, or Archbishops make a profession of faith in the first synod or council they attend after their consecration is a purely disciplinary law. It must be considered to have lost its binding force, therefore, or rather to have been merged in the more sweeping provisions of the above-quoted law.[33]

Macmillan Co., 1932), p. 114, relates that at the Third Provincial Council of Baltimore, held in 1837, "the customary profession of faith was made by those Bishops who were present for the first time."

[31] "In actis synodi legitur fidei professionem emisisse iuxta symbolum pii PP. IV Episcopos prima vice praesentes. Etsi vero ad legis rigorem satis esse videatur, ut fidei professionem soli illi emittant Antistites, qui eam in anteactis Synodis nondum emiserint; cum tamen usu constanti receptum sit ut ab omnibus Concilii Patribus semper fiat, idcirco Sacra Congregatio optat, ut in futuris Conciliis Episcopi omnes fidem iuxta formulam Pii IV absque ullo discrimine profiteantur."—S. C. de Prop. Fide., 8 maii 1860.

[32] Canon 6, 6°. "Si qua ex ceteris disciplinaribus legibus, quae usque adhuc viguerunt, nec explicite nec implicite in Codice contineatur, ea vim omnem amisisse dicenda est, nisi in probatis liturgicis libris reperiatur, aut lex sit iuris divini sive positivi sive naturalis."

[33] When the canons of the present law were being compiled, it was the intention of the authorities in charge to preserve all the disciplinary laws of the Council of Trent in the Code, but this idea was abandoned before its promulgation.—Cf. Van Hove, *Commentarium Lovaniense in Codicem Iuris Canonici* (vol. I, tom. II, *De Legibus Ecclesiasticis,* Mechliniae-Romae: H. Dessain, 1930), II, 75; Vidal, "Il Nuovo Codice di Diritto Canonico," *Civilta Cattolica,* anno 68 (1917), vol. II, 557.

Article III. Prelates and Dignitaries

A. *Cardinals*

Canon 1406.—§ 1. Obligatione emittendi professionem fidei . . . tenentur:

2°. Coram Sacri Collegi Decano, Cardinalibus primis in ordine presbyterorum et diaconorum et S.R.E. camerario, promoti ad cardinalitiam dignitatem;

The provision for those promoted to the Cardinalate to make a profession of faith is not new to universal ecclesiastical legislation. There was provision made for this procedure by the Council of Trent in the session that prescribed that a profession of faith be made by all candidates for the Episcopacy and the Cardinate (Sess. xxiv *de ref.*, cap. 1).

The Dean of the College of Cardinals is the oldest in promotion to a suburbican see of Rome.[34] The *first Cardinal Priest* and the *first Cardinal Deacon* spoken of by the Code in this canon are relative terms, for it is evidently in the mind of the legislator that the profession take place in Rome[35] before the first Cardinal Priest and the first Cardinal Deacon *"inter actu praesentes in Curia,"*[36] as it would be manifestly impossible to make the profession if the senior Cardinal Priest was Archbishop elsewhere and was resident in his see when the profession was to be made.

The fourth member of the College of Cardinals who should be present when a newly created member makes his profession of faith is the Cardinal Camerlengo of the Holy Roman Church, he who has the care and administration of the temporal goods of the Apostolic See, especially during the time of a vacancy.[37]

The tenor of the legislation is that a profession of faith need not be made separately before each of the four individual members of the College listed above, but before the assembled group in convocation for the very purpose of receiving the profession of the new member to their ranks.

[34] Cf. Canon 237, § 1.

[35] Canon 234 provides that if the person who is promoted to the dignity of the Cardinalate is not in Rome, he must, upon receiving the red biretta that signifies the honor he has received, take an oath that he will go to see the Supreme Pontiff within one year, unless this is impossible.

[36] Cf. Blat, *Commentarium,* III, 423.

[37] Cf. Canon 262.

B. *Bishops, Abbots and Prelates nullius, Vicars and Prefects Apostolic*

Canon 1406.—§ 1, 3°. Coram delegato ab Apostolica Sede promoti ad sedem episcopalem etiam non residentialem, vel ad regimen Abbatiae vel Praelaturae nullius, Vicariatus Apostolici, Praefecturae Apostolicae;

In a previous historical chapter the obligation of Bishops to make a profession of faith has been discussed. Indeed, such discipline, as has been noted, is of very early origin.[38] The law re-stated in the Code is that promulgated by Pope Gregory XIV in the constitution, *Onus Apostolicae,* issued May 15, 1591.[39] This Pontiff ruled that those candidates who were being considered for the episcopacy were to make their profession of faith before that prelate who had been deputed by the Holy See to make an inquiry into the faith, morals, learning, and prudence of the candidate. The latter might also make the profession before one who had been subdelegated by the prelate to make the inquiry. The profession, according to the instructions of the Pontiff, was to be made before a notary public and witnesses, the document to be signed both by the one who made the inquiry and the candidate. The document, sealed, was to be sent to the Holy See in its authentic form.[40] It is to be noted that this legislation seemed to provide for a profession of faith from those who were being considered for the episcopacy. Today a profession is demanded only from the one who has actually been chosen, for the Code prescribes that those promoted to the episcopacy must make a profession of faith to the delegate appointed for that purpose by the Holy See before their canonical institution.[41] Coronata insists that the profession must be made to the delegate appointed by the Holy See before the one who has been promoted to the episcopacy has received the Apostolic bulls announcing the conferring of his title.[42] The formula is to be found in the *Pontificale Romanum.*[43]

[38] Cf. article on the *Liber Diurnus,* pp. 18-23.

[39] Cf. *Fontes,* n. 171.

[40] Cf. Grandclaude, *Ius Canonicum Juxta Ordinem Decretalium Recentioribus Sedis Apostolicae Decretis et Rectae Rationi in Omnibus Consonium* (3 vols., Parisiis, 1882), 118, 119; Wernz, *Ius Decretalium,* III, n. 14; Reiffenstuel, *Ius Canonicum,* I, 89, n. 156; Schmalzgrueber, *Ius Ecclesiasticum Universum* (5 vols, in 12, Romae, 1843-1845), I, 173, ad 7.

[41] Canon 332, § 2. "Ante canonicam institutionem seu provisionem candidatus, praeter fidei professionem de qua in can. 1406-1408, iusiurandum fidelitatis erga Sanctam Sedem edat . . ."

[42] *Institutiones* II, 472.

[43] Cf. tit. *De Consecratione electi in Episcopum.* In Catholic states together with the profession of faith and the oath of fealty to the Holy See, there is

There is no distinction made between residential and non-residential Bishops with regard to the obligation of profession, therefore Coadjutors, Auxiliaries, and merely Titular Bishops must make a profession of faith before their institution. The obligation is grave and personal, but its omission does not effect that the institution is invalid, for the Code does not make the obligation a condition *sine qua non* for canonical institution or expressly state that the act is invalid if the profession of faith is omitted.[44] The penalties for non-compliance with the law will be discussed in a later chapter of this work.

Auxiliaries and Coadjutors, even those with right of succession, must make another profession of faith whenever they are transferred, promoted or succeed to another see, according to the rule of canon 1406, § 2,[45] for such transfer, promotion, or succession is the obtaining of a new office. The same obligation seems also to hold for residential Bishops who are promoted or transferred and for those Bishops who upon their resignation are named Titular Bishops or Archbishops. Such appointment is a new dignity and is governed by the same legislation as pertains in the cases mentioned above.

Those prelates who rule over the clergy and people of a district that is separated from every other diocese—Abbots *nullius* if their church is an abbey, and Prelates *nullius* if their church is a secular prelacy—are governed as to profession of faith as are Bishops, i. e., before they take office they must make a profession of faith before one who has been delegated to receive it by the Holy See.[46] The reason for this legislation is that such prelates are truly Ordinaries in the government of priests and people; they are nominated and instituted, or confirmed, by the Roman Pontiff, and must have the same qualifications as the law requires for Bishops.[47] It is fitting, therefore, that they are required to make the same protestation of orthodoxy as do the Bishops of the Holy Roman Church.

Because the Holy See reserves to itself exclusively the nomination of Vicars and Prefects Apostolic, i. e., those who govern territories

added an oath of fidelity to the Catholic king.—Cf. Coronata, *Institutiones,* II, 472, nota 6.

[44] Canon 11. "Irritantes aut inhabilitantes eae tantum leges habendae sunt, quibus aut actum esse nullum aut inhabilem esse personam expresse vel aequivalenter statuitur."

[45] "Qui priore dimisso aliud officium vel beneficium aut dignitatem etiam eiusdem speciei consequuntur, rursus debent fidei professionem emittere . . ."

[46] Canon 319 defines the function of these prelates in the Church.

[47] Cf. canon 320.

which are not erected into dioceses,[48] the Code demands that the latter also make a profession of faith before a delegate of the Apostolic See.

It must be remembered that all of the Bishops, Abbots and Prelates *nullius,* and Vicars and Prefects Apostolic may also make their profession before the one who has been subdelegated by the delegate appointed by the Holy See. This is indicated in the *Onus Apostolicae* of Pope Gregory XIV,[49] and is according to the general principle of the subdelegation of power, treated by the Code in canon 199, § 2. This law declares that jurisdiction delegated by the Holy See can be subdelegated either for one act or even habitually, unless the first person was delegated for personal qualifications, or subdelegation is forbidden.[50] There is usually no qualification on the delegation given by the Holy See to receive the profession of faith from the prelates spoken of in this article; the power, therefore, may be subdelegated.[51]

C. *Vicars General*

Canon 1406.—§ 1. Obligatione emittendi professionem fidei . . . tenentur:

7°. Coram loci Ordinario eiusve delegato, Vicarius Generalis . . . ;

The Code enjoins the Bishop to choose a Vicar General under certain circumstances, namely, when this is necessary for the right government of a diocese.[52] Since the law is silent on the formalities regarding the appointment, it is safe to assume that the ordinary power given to a Vicar General comes to him when he accepts the office. The legislation under discussion demands a profession of faith from the holder of this office without specifying the time of the profession. While it is true that the Council of Trent gave a period

[48] Cf. canon 293, § 1.

[49] "Si . . . qui professionem emissurus est, a praelato inquirente longe distet, tunc enim is praelatus ex subdelegatione inquirentis, professionem admittere debebit cui promovendus vicinior erit . . ."—*Fontes,* n. 171.

[50] "Etiam potestas iurisdictionis ab Apostolica Sede delegata subdelegari potest sive ad actum, sive etiam habitualiter, nisi electa fuerit industria personae aut subdelegatio prohibita."

[51] Cf. Blat, *Commentarium,* III, 423.

[52] Canon 366, § 1.

of two months' grace to beneficiaries before they had to make a profession of faith, this no longer holds, as is clearly indicated by a reply of the Sacred Congregation of the Council.[53] Because, moreover, the whole tenor of the canon is that those promoted to designated offices or dignities make the profession before they assume their office, or in the act of taking over the duties of their office, it is more probable that the Vicar General should make his profession of faith before the local Ordinary or his delegate before exercising the duties of his office.

It is provided by law that in the case of a diocese having many diverse rites or a large number of parishes the Bishop may constitute more than one Vicar General.[54] In the latter case, a newly appointed Vicar General might make the required profession of faith before one of the other Vicar Generals, or their delegates, for the canon demands merely that the profession be taken before the Ordinary of the place, which term is governed by the prescriptions of canon 198, § 2, and includes besides the Bishop also the Vicar General of a diocese.

Just as a Bishop might delegate a priest to receive the profession of faith from a newly appointed Vicar General, so might an already existing Vicar General appoint a priest to receive the profession of a new prelate of the same rank, supposing that the new Vicar General chose to fulfill his obligation before the already appointed Vicar General rather than before the Bishop. The Code seems to permit the utmost freedom in the selection of the local Ordinary, or his delegate, before whom the obligation is to be fulfilled.

In the event of the resignation of a Vicar General or the expiration of his jurisdiction by reason of revocation of his appointment by his Bishop or by the suspension or revocation of the Bishop's own jurisdiction, the Vicar General would have to make another profession of faith before the same or another Bishop if he were to be reappointed, for the prescriptions of canon 1406, § 2, would then hold.

D. *Vicars Capitular*

Canon 1406.—§ 1. Obligatione emittendi professionem fidei . . . tenentur:

4°. Coram Capitulo cathedrali, Vicarius Capitularis;

[53] *AAS,* III (1911), 134.

[54] Cf. canon 366, § 3.

In case of a vacancy the government of a diocese devolves on the Cathedral chapter, unless there is an Apostolic Administrator or the Holy See has arranged otherwise.[55] The law provides that within eight days from the notice of the vacancy of the episcopal see the Cathedral chapter must elect a Vicar Capitular for the government of a diocese.[56] Now, the jurisdiction of the Vicar Capitular depends as much on the profession of faith that he must take upon assuming his office as it does on his election, for it is not until after he has made his profession of faith before the other members of the chapter that he receives jurisdiction for governing the diocese.[57] The wording of canon 438, which demands that the Vicar Capitular make a profession of faith before he assumes jurisdiction, is such that it seems to demand the profession as an essential requisite for the exercise of the jurisdiction, so necessary that if it were omitted all the acts of the Vicar Capitular in the exercise of his office would be null and void.[58] Despite the assertion of some canonists of note that the clause, *"edita fidei professione,"* which is found in canon 438, is not conditional and establishes only a point of time in a non-conditional sense, hence does not affect the jurisdiction itself,[59] the sense of the wording of the canon seems to be clear that the jurisdiction is dependent on the profession. If this were not so, it would be impossible to determine the moment in which the Vicar Capitular receives his jurisdiction, for the Code certainly does not say that his election confers jurisdiction

[55] Cf. canon 431.

[56] Cf. canon 432, § 1.

[57] Canon 438. "Vicarius Capitularis, edita fidei professione de qua in can. 1406-1408, statim iurisdictionem obtinet, quin necessaria sit ullius confirmatio."

[58] "Professio fidei videtur, ob modum loquendi Codicis, 'edita fidei professione . . . statim obtinet,' condicio sine qua non iurisdictionis obtinendae."—Vermeersch-Creusen, *Epitome,* I, 385; cf. De Meester, *Compendium,* II, 237.

[59] Cf. Augustine, *A Commentary,* II, 491. This author seems to be confused on the issue. After stating that in his opinion the clause in question is not conditional and does not affect the jurisdiction, he goes on to affirm: "However, in view of the importance attached to the profession and its being placed before *'iurisdictionem obtinet,'* we may conclude that the *ratio legis* lays stress on the profession, and this would seem to imply that it is a *conditio sine qua non."* Coronata holds that the profession of faith is not a *conditio sine qua non.—Institutiones,* I, 556. Cf. Van Hove, *Commentarium Lovaniense in Codicem Iuris Canonici* (vol. I, tom. IV, *De Rescriptis,* Mechliniae-Romae: H. Dessain, 1936), IV, 123, in which this author contends that the use of the ablative absolute indicates an accidental clause, not an essential one. Today the presumption stands that the use of the ablative absolute does not regularly imply the same significance as do the particles, "si" and "dummodo." Cf. Vermeersch-Creusen, *Epitome,* I, 145; Michiels, *Normae Generales Juris Canonici* (2 vols., Lubin, Palonia: Universitas Catholica, 1929), II, 217.

automatically, and it certainly does affirm that the Vicar Capitular needs no confirmation once he has made the required profession of faith.[60]

This is the only indication in the whole legislation on the subject of profession of faith that the profession is an essential for obtaining jurisdiction. In all other cases profession of faith is demanded, indeed, and its no-fulfillment is punished by penalties, but it is not an essential condition for obtaining jurisdiction in the office, duty, or dignity to which a cleric is appointed.

Augustine contends that in this country, since the diocesan consultors take the place of the Cathedral chapter, the diocesan administrator who is elected by the consultors when the see becomes vacant must make a profession of faith before the consultors as a body.[61] There is no doubt that he is correct in this assertion. The Code in canon 427 provides that where a Cathedral chapter cannot be established, a body of diocesan consultors shall be set up; and that the same canons that hold for the government of a diocese by a Cathedral chapter must also be interpreted as applying to the consultors.[62] That diocesan consultors in the United States have the right to elect an administrator of a diocese is evident from a reply of the Pontifical Commission for the Interpretation of the Code that where there are at least five or six diocesan consultors, they elect the administrator.[63] The Commission declared, furthermore, that the provisions of the II and III Plenary Councils of Baltimore on the right to name an administrator of a diocese[64] no longer hold in this country.[65] Whenever there occurs a vacancy in an episcopal see, there-

[60] Cf. Blat, *Commentarium* (I, *Normae Generales,* Romae, 1921), I, 409.

[61] Cf. *A Commentary,* VI, 487.

[62] "Coetus consultorum dioecesanorum vices Capituli cathedralis, qua episcopi senatus, supplet; quare quae canones ad gubernationem dioecesis, sive plena sive ea impedita aut vacante, Capitulo cathedrali tribuunt, ea de coetu quoque consultorum dioecesanorum intelligendia sunt."

[63] Cf. *AAS,* XI, 75; Bouscaren, *Canon Law Digest* (2 vols., 2 supplements, Milwaukee: Bruce, 1934-1941), I (1934), 242-243; Woywod, *A Practi-Commentary on the Code of Canon Law* (2 vols., 5. ed., New York: Wagner, 1939), I, 155; II, 566.

[64] *Concilii Plenarii Baltimorensis II Acta et Decreta* (Baltimorae, 1894), nn. 96-99; *Acta et Decreta Concilii Plenarii Baltimorensis III* (Baltimorae, 1894), n. 22. The Councils provided the right of Bishops to name an administrator of a diocese *mortis causa.*

[65] Cf. *AAS,* XI, 75.

fore, the consultors should elect one to administer the diocese. Whenever he makes a profession of faith after election, before them assembled in a body, he receives full jurisdiction.[66]

E. *Those Promoted to Dignities or Canonries*

Canon 1406.—§ 1. Obligatione emittendi professionem fidei . . . tenentur:

5°. Coram loci Ordinario eiusve delegato et coram Capitulo, qui ad dignitatem vel canonicatum promoti sunt;

The Council of Trent, as has been indicated in an earlier chapter of this work,[67] provided that those promoted to canonries or dignities in cathedral churches were bound to make a profession of faith not only before the Bishop or his delegate but also before the chapter.[68] It is evident that the Code has changed this legislation but little. Because the words, "Ordinary of the place," have been substituted for "Bishop," however, the profession of those promoted to dignities or canonries can be made also to the Vicar General, or a delegate of the latter, in a residential see or in an abbacy or prelature *nullius*.[69] The profession should be made, as has been indicated with regard to the Vicar General, before the canonry or dignity is conferred, or in the act of assuming the office or dignity. The period of grace has been abrogated. The fact that the present legislation, moreover, does not qualify the term, "canonry," indicates that collegiate as well as cathedral canons must make a profession of faith before they take possession. This opinion is strengthened by the wording of the Code in canon 405, § 2, which speaks of all canonries without distinction.[70] It must be concluded, therefore, that profession of faith is now demanded of all canons, either cathedral or collegiate.[71]

[66] Cf. Woywod, *loc. cit.*

[67] Cf. p. 35.

[68] Sess. XXIV *de ref.*, cap. 12.

[69] Cf. canon 198, § 2; Blat, *Commentarium,* III, 424.

[70] "De fidei professione ab ipsis ante captam professionem emittenda servetur praescriptum can. 1406-1408." After the Tridentine legislation on the profession of faith required of canons, there arose doubts as to the obligation of collegiate canons to make the profession. In answering these doubts, the Sacred Congregation of the Council repeatedly affirmed that the obligation extended only to the cathedral canons, that the collegiate canons were exempt. This was the common teaching of canonists until the promulgation of the Code. Cf. Benedict XIV, *Institutiones Ecclesiasticae* (Romae, 1747), n. LX; Grandclaude, *Ius Canonicum,* I, 119; Reiffenstuel, *Ius Canonicum,* I, 90-91.

[71] Cf. Augustine, *A Commentary,* VI, 488; Blat, *Commentarium,* III, 424.

Canon 1406, § 1, 5°, also demands that a profession of faith be taken by those who are promoted to dignities. To contend that the term is meant to be all inclusive and to embrace even those who are honored by the Holy See by being created Papal Chamberlains, Domestic Prelates, or Protonotaries is to misunderstand the legislation. Since the present discipline is merely that of the Council of Trent in slightly altered form, it follows that the dignities spoken of are only those of the old law. Now the old law meant the term, "dignity," to refer only to certain positions of prominence in a chapter of canons. The Code itself, refraining from specifying the various dignities of a chapter, distinguishes these dignities in general from canonries and affirms merely that among the holders of both positions the various duties of a chapter are distributed.[72] Although the dignities are established by custom or by particular statute, the more common of them include the offices of Presiding Officer, Dean, Archdeacon, and Archpriest. [73] It is of the candidates for these dignities alone that the Code speaks in canon 1406, § 1, 5°, demanding that they make a profession of faith before or in the act of taking possession of their office.

The legislation under consideration demands that those promoted to dignities or canonries must make their profession of faith both before the Ordinary of the place or his delegate and before the chapter. The profession is usually made before both at the same time, i. e., before the local Ordinary or his delegate and the chapter, but it need not necessarily be made thus, for the wording of the canon does not imply that a profession made first before the Ordinary or his delegate and then the chapter, or vice versa, would be invalid, or even illicit.[74] Commentators on the pre-Code legislation regarding this prescription, which is the same as the discipline of the Code, discussed, moreover, the validity of a profession made before a chapter of which the Bishop or his delegate was a canon. They all declared that such a profession of faith was admissible and that it need not be repeated before the Bishop or his delegate.[75] This is indirect argument, at least, that the mind of the legislator is simply this: A profession of faith must be made by those promoted to dignities or canonries before the Bishop

[72] Canon 393, § 1. "In qualibet ecclesia capitulari sint dignitates et canonici inter quos varia officia distribuantur . . ."

[73] Cf. De Meester, *Iuris Canonici Compendium,* II, 198-199; Wernz, *Ius Decretalium,* II, nn. 771-778.

[74] Augustine *(A Commentary, VI, 488)* writes as follows: "We say: 'at the same time,' for if the bishop or his delegate . . . is not present when the profession is made before the chapter, it would have to be made again."

[75] Cf. Reiffenstuel, *Ius Canonicum,* I, 92; Grandclaude, *Ius Canonicum,* I, 120.

or his delegate *and* before the chapter. It makes no difference whether this profession is made before the Bishop or his delegate and the chapter meeting together, or before each separately.[76]

It has been decided in a response of the Sacred Congregation of the Council that if the profession is made before a chapter at which the delegate of the Bishop is present as a member of the chapter, and he inscribes his name to the document of profession merely as a member of it, omitting mention of his official capacity, the profession is nevertheless valid.[77] It is also necessary, according to another response, that the chapter of canons as such must be present to accept the profession. It is not enough that it be made before the member with the greatest dignity or who has precedence because of age.[78] This is not to say, however, that the full complement of canons must be present in order that the profession be valid. It would seem sufficient if the absolute majority were present, for canon 101, § 1, 1°, which is analogous to the present question, rules that unless the common law or particular statute prescribes a different course of action, that which has been voted for by the absolute majority of those who vote shall have force in law.

The obligation of making the profession of faith both before the local Ordinary or his delegate and the chapter is so grave that in the case of a see's becoming vacant before the one promoted to a dignity or canonry could make the necessary profession, it would have to be made before the Vicar Capitular and the chapter, either before one and the other separately or before both meeting together, as has been described above.[79] This would also be true if instead of a Vicar Capitular there would be another appointed by the Holy See to administer a diocese during a vacancy. In this latter case, the profession would have to be made before the administrator and the chapter.

The only restriction placed by the Code on the one who may be delegated by the local Ordinary to receive the profession of faith from those promoted to dignities or canonries is that he must be a cleric. Augustine contends that the delegate should be an ecclesiastical dignitary,[80] but this

[76] Cf. Blat, *Commentarium,* III, 424. Coronata (*Institutiones,* II, 350) holds that a two-fold profession of faith is demanded if the Ordinary or his delegate is not present when the profession is made before the chapter.

[77] S.C.C., *Sarzanen,* 14 ian. 1679, ad 1—*Fontes,* n. 2847.

[78] S.C.C., 7 aug. 1683—*Fontes,* n. 2871.

[79] Cf. Reiffenstuel, *Ius Canonicum,* I, 82.

[80] Cf. *A Commentary,* VI, 488.

opinion is prompted, no doubt, by a feeling about the fitness of things rather than by any legislation on the subject, although the Sacred Consistorial Congregation has suggested that in a council or a synod the one delegated by the Bishop to receive the profession of faith should be endowed with some ecclesiastical dignity.[81] This does not mean, however, that the local Ordinary could not delegate any cleric to receive the profession of faith. According to the present legislation the Ordinary needs no particular reason for delegating this duty, for the law places no restrictions on the reception of profession of faith. As a matter af fact, it provides specifically for a delegate, thereby, at least implicitly, giving the local Ordinary the utmost freedom in the matter. This is in contrast to the old law, which placed a personal obligation on the Bishop or his Vicar, if the former were impeded, to receive the profession.[82]

The Council of Trent gave a period of two months' grace before those promoted to dignities or canonries had to make a profession of faith. In other words, the one so promoted could take possession of his office and receive the fruits therefrom for two months before the injunction to make a confession of faith bound under penalty of losing those fruits.[83] This no longer obtains, for the Sacred Congregation of the Council in a reply given March 1, 1911, declared that in the future the profession of faith must be made before those promoted take possession of office.[84]

F. *Prelates of the Roman Curia*

It is not provided in the Code that certain prelates of the Roman Curia make a profession of faith before they take possession of office, but Pope Pius XI in an Apostolic constitution, *Ad incrementum*, dated August 15, 1934, ruled as follows:

1. After they have received their letters of appointment Protonotaries Apostolic must make their profession before the whole college of Protonotaries Apostolic, or, in certain extraordinary cases, before at least two members of that college who have been delegated to receive the profession.

[81] Cf. *AAS*, II, 857; Coronata, *Institutiones*, II, 349.

[82] Cf. S.C.C., *Calaguritana*, 22 sept. 1696—*Fontes*, n. 2954.

[83] Sess. XXIV *de ref.*, cap. 12.

[84] *AAS*, III, 134.

2. Auditors of the Rota must make a profession of faith before the whole Rotal college on the day on which they are accepted into it.

3. The clerics of the Apostolic Camera must make their profession of faith before the presiding Cardinal.

4. The *Prelati Votantes* of the Signatura Apostolica must make a profession of faith before the entire Rotal college.

5. *Prelati Referendarii* (consultors) of the Signatura Apostolica must make their profession of faith before the Cardinal prefect of that body, the secretary, the dean, and the *Prelati Votantes.*[85]

G. *Diocesan Consultors*

> *Canon 1406.—§ 1. Obligatione emittendi professionem fidei . . . tenentur:*
>
> 6°. *Coram loci Ordinario eiusve delegato et coram aliis consultoribus, assumpti ad officium consultorum dioecesanorum;*

The regulation demanding that a profession of faith be taken before the local Ordinary or his delegate by all promoted to be diocesan consultors is new with the Code. There was no provision made for consultors in the pre-Code legislation, which, in fact, did not acknowledge their existence. It is very probable that the institution of consultors is a result of the Plenary Councils of Baltimore. Augustine says:

> The Fathers of these councils realized, on the one hand, that . . . ecclesiastical funds were not in a condition to permit the establishment of regular chapters, and, on the other hand, many of the Bishops were overburdened with work. Hence the appeal of the II Plenary Council for helpers and counsellors on whom the Bishops might unload a part of their burden.[86]

Canon 427 defines in a general way the functions of the diocesan consultors. This body, which acts as sort of Bishop's senate, takes the place of the Cathedral chapter. Whatever is attributed by the canons to the Cathedral chapter in relation to the government of a

[85] Cf. *AAS,* XXVI, 497—521; *Apollinaris* (Romae, 1928—), VIII, 14, 18, 22, 25, 28.

[86] *A Commentary,* II, 463.

diocese, either co-operating with the Bishop or during the vacancy of a see, also applies to the diocesan consultors as a body.[87]

It is to be noted that, as in the case of those promoted to dignities or canonries, those appointed consultors must make their profession of faith both before the local Ordinary or his delegate *and* the other consultors. This may be done at the same time or a two-fold profession made, one before the Ordinary or his delegate and the other before the other consultors, as was held in the case of canons.[88] Usually the consultors meet in a convenient place with the local Ordinary, and the one promoted to the dignity makes his profession before them.[89] If one or two of the consultors are absent from the meeting, it would not affect the validity of the profession, as was indicated in the case of the chapter.[90] All that the law requires is that a *"coetus"* (body) of consultors be present, and this condition would be verified if the majority of the members was present.

Because the legislation of the Code requires that the profession be made before the local Ordinary, the Vicar General could validly receive the profession of faith of a newly appointed consultor, as could the delegate appointed by the Vicar General.[91] This delegate, as well as the one appointed by a Bishop to receive the profession, could be any cleric, but here again, as has been noted in another portion of this work, [92] the delegate should be one who is endowed with some ecclesiastical dignity. There is nothing to prevent the local Ordinary from naming one of the consultors to receive the profession from a new member.

The Code provides that the consultors shall remain in office for three years and declares that they can be reappointed for another term.[93] In this latter case the profession would have to be repeated

[87] ". . . quae canones ad gubernationem dioecesis . . . Capitulo cathedrali tribuunt, ea de coetu quoque consultorum dioecesanorum intelligenda sunt."

[88] Cf. Blat, *Commentarium,* III, 424; Wernz-Vidal, *Ius Canonicum* (IV, *De Rebus,* Romae: Apud Aedes Universitatis Gregorianae, 1935), IV, 22, in nota 39.

[89] Cf. Augustine, *A Commentary,* VI, 488.

[90] Cf. p. 75, *supra.*

[91] Cf. canon 198, § 2. Cf. p. 73, *supra,* as to profession made by canons before the Vicar General or his delegate.

[92] Cf. p. 63, *supra.*

[93] Cf. canon 426, §§ 1, 2.

upon reappointment, for the prescriptions of canon 1406, § 2, would then hold.[94]

What is said about diocesan consultors in this discussion does not apply to the so-called parish priest consultors spoken of by the Code in canon 385.[95] It cannot be affirmed, moreover, that profession of faith is necessary to the validity of the appointment of a diocesan consultor, for the Code does not make a contrary act invalid; thus the prescriptions of canon 11 must hold.[96] The penalties that may be inflicted on a diocesan consultor who does not make the required profession of faith will be discussed in a later chapter.

Article IV. Pastors and Those Promoted to Benefices to Which Is Attached the Care of Souls

Canon 1406.—§ 1. Obligatione emittendi professionem fidei . . . tenentur:

7°. Coram loci Ordinario eiusve delegato . . . parochi et ii quibus provisum fuit de beneficiis quibusvis, etiam manualibus, curam animarium habentibus;

The Council of Trent provided that those named to benefices to which was attached the care of souls must within two months of taking possession of their office make a profession of faith before the Bishop or his Vicar or *Officialis*.[97] The present legislation, while more specific, is substantially the prescription of the Council of Trent, although there is a change in the persons to whom the profession can be made and the two months' period of grace that was formerly given is now abolished, as canon 461 specifically states that the profession of faith must be made either before or in the very act of taking possession of a parish.[98]

[94] Canon 1406, § 2. "Qui, priore dimisso, aliud officium vel beneficium aut dignitatem etiam eiusdem speciei consequuntur, rursus debent fidei professionem emittere ad normam huius canonis."

[95] Canon 385, § 1. "In quavis dioecesi habeantur examinatores synodales et parochi consultores . . ."

[96] Canon 11. "Irritantes aut inhabilitantes eae tantum leges habendae sunt, quibus aut actum esse nullum aut inhabilem esse personam expresse vel aequivalenter statuitur."

[97] Cf. sess, XXIV *de ref.*, cap. 12.

[98] Canon 461: "Curam animarum parochus obtinet a momento captae possessionis ad normam can. 1443-1445; et ante possessionem aut in ipso possessionis capiendae actu fidei professionem edere debet, de qua in can. 1406, § 1, n. 7."

In order adequately to understand the obligation of making a profession of faith by those to whom are assigned parishes or chapels or other benefices to which the care of souls is attached, the legal meaning of the term, "pastor," must be understood. According to the Code, a pastor is a priest to whom a parish has been given in title with the obligation of caring for the souls therein, under the authority of the local Ordinary.[99] But the law also includes as pastors those priests who are called "quasi pastors," [100] namely those priests who are assigned to parishes in apostolic vicariates and prefectures. Considered as pastors in law also are parochial vicars who have full parochial powers.[101] These latter include the *vicarius curatus* (vicar), the *vicarius oeconimus* (parish administrator), *vicarius substitutus* (substitute), and the *vicarius adiutor* (adjutant). In general they are those priests who in the name and place of the pastor perform the parochial duties in the care of souls and in celebrating the Divine office.[102] While pastors and quasi-pastors are obliged to make a profession of faith upon taking office, the obligation of parochial vicars is not so definite and corresponds to the parochial power they exercise. It will be necessary, therefore, to consider each one specifically:

(a) If a parish is united *pleno iure* (in full right) to a religious house, to a Cathedral or collegiate chapter, or any other moral person, a vicar (*vicarius curatus*) must be appointed for the actual care of souls, and to him belongs their exclusive care, with all the rights and duties as defined by the common law, by diocesan statutes, or by legitimate custom.[103] Since he has all the rights and obligations of a pastor,[104] that is, the *full parochial power* spoken of in canon 451, § 2, 2°, he is bound to make a profession of faith either before or upon taking possession of his office.

[99] Canon 451, § 1: "Parochus est sacerdos vel persona moralis cui paroecia collata est in titulum cum cura animarum sub Ordinarii loci auctoritate exercenda."

[100] Canon 451, § 2, 1°: "Parochis aequiparantur cum omnibus iuribus et obligationibus paroecialibus et parochorum nomine in iure veniunt: Quasi-parochi, qui quasi-paroecias regunt, de quibus in can. 216, § 3."

[101] Canon 451, § 2, 2°. "Parochis aequiparantur . . . et parochorum in iure veniunt: Vicarii paroeciales, si plena potestate paroeciali sint praediti."

[102] Wernz-Vidal, *Ius Canonicum* (II, *De Personis*, 2. ed., Romae: Apud Aedes Universitatis Gregorianae, 1928), II, 424.

[103] Cf. canon 471, §§ 1 and 4; cf. also canon 1425.

[104] Woywod, *A Practical Commentary*, I, 171.

(b) Administrators of parishes (*vicarii oeconomi*) are those appointed during the vacancy of a parish to supply for the pastor until such a one is appointed.[105] *Per se* the administrator is obliged to the fulfillment of all parochial duties and has all the rights of a pastor.[106] He has, therefore, the full parochial power spoken of in canon 451, § 2, 2°, and is to be considered as a pastor. He is, on these grounds, obliged to make a profession of faith as is the pastor.[107]

(c) Substitutes (*vicarii substituti*) are those who have been legitimately constituted to perform the parochial duties, either because the pastor is absent for a period exceeding a week, or because the pastor, having been deprived of his parish, is appealing his case to the Holy See.[108] In the event, of course, that the parochial power of the substitute is curtailed either by the pastor or the Ordinary of the place, as is provided in canon 474, [109] he need not make a profession of faith, for he would not have full parochial power and would not be embraced under the provisions of canon 451, § 2, 2°.[110] Normally there is a restriction of the power of a substitute made by the pastor who obtains his services or by the local Ordinary, particularly as to the rights of revenue. Certainly this would be true in the case of a pastor who calls in a neighboring priest to take care of his parish during a few days' absence. It seems, therefore, that only in extraordinary circumstances would the profession of faith have to be made by a substitute, as, for example, when the pastor who has been deprived of his parish is appealing his case to the Holy See,[111] and a substitute has been appointed.[112]

(d) Adjutants (*vicarii adiutores*) are those who have been deputed by the local Ordinary to assume the duties of a pastor who, on account of some permanent cause, e.g., old age, mental debility, blindness, etc.,

[105] Cf. canon 471, § 2.

[106] Cf. canon 473, § 1. "Vicarius oeconomus iisdem iuribus gaudet iisdemque oficiis adstringitur, ac parochus, in iis quae animarum curam spectant . . ."

[107] Cf. Wernz-Vidal, *Ius Canonicum,* II, 799; *AAS*, VIII, 129.

[108] Cf. canon 474.

[109] "Vicarius substitutus qui constituitur . . . locum parochi tenet in omnibus quae ad curam animarum spectant, nisi Ordinarius loci vel parochus aliquid exceperint."

[110] Wernz-Vidal, *op. cit.,* 800.

[111] Cf. canon 1923, § 2.

[112] Cf. Wernz-Vidal, *loc. cit.*

is not able satisfactorily to conduct the affairs of the parish with their corresponding obligations.[113] The adjutant's parochial powers are to be measured according to the terms of this appointment. He may be appointed to take the place of the pastor in all the affairs of the parish and have all the rights and duties of a pastor, with the exception of applying Mass for the congregation, which obligation rests with the pastor.[114] It does not seem that the limitation with regard to the application of Mass for the congregation is sufficient to take away the *full parochial power* that would classify the vicar adjutant among those who are called pastors. This opinion is strengthened by a response of the Sacred Consistorial Congregation that rectors of certain churches and chapels have the same care of souls as pastors, although they do not have the obligation of applying the *missa pro populo*.[115] It follows, then, that such adjutants who are appointed with all the rights and duties of a pastor, with the exception noted, must make a profession of faith when they take over their office.[116]

A vicar adjutant may be appointed, however, without full parochial powers, in which case his rights and obligations must be learned from his letter of appointment.[117] In this case he would certainly not have to make a profession of faith when he assumes office.[118]

(e) Assistants (*vicarii cooperatores*) are those who aid the pastor in the administration of the parochial duties.[119] Since their rights and duties depend on the diocesan statutes, the Bishop's letter of appointment, and the commission of the pastor, [120] they cannot be said to have full parochial power. They are not, therefore, bound to a profession of faith upon their appointment.

Whether military chaplains can be classed as pastors with full parochial powers, must be judged by the prescriptions of the Holy See,

[113] Cf. canon 475, § 1.

[114] Cf. canon 475, § 2.

[115] Cf. *AAS*, XI (1919), 340.

[116] The adjutant who supplies in all things has ordinary jurisdiction to hear Confessions; he may delegate another priest to assist at marriages; he may dispense from matrimonial impediments, even in the external forum, according to canon 1044.—Cf. Vermeersch-Creusen, *Epitome*, I, 413.

[117] Canon 475, § 2. ". . . si vero suppleat ex parte dumtaxat, eius iura et obligationes desumantur ex litteris deputationis."

[118] Cf. Wernz-Vidal, *op. cit.*, 802.

[119] Cf. canon 476.

[120] Cf. canon 476, § 6; Wernz-Vidal, *op cit.*, 804.

which sets up the military ordinariate.[121] There seems to be no restriction on the power of such chaplains in the United States, at least with regard to their own subjects.[122] They do not seem, therefore, exempt from the obligation of making a profession of faith when they take up their duties with the army or navy.

Besides pastors, those who have been appointed to any benefice, even though it is only manual, to which is attached the care of souls, must make a profession of faith. Manual, temporal, or removable benefices, according to canon 1411, 4, are those which are bestowed subject to the will of the one who makes the appointment. A benefice is a juridical entity permanently established by competent authority and consisting of a sacred office and the right of receiving the revenues from the endowment attached thereto.[123]

Included in the category of those who are appointed to benefices to which is attached the care of souls are rectors of churches spoken of in canon 479, § 1,[124] who actually do enjoy a benefice and a certain care of souls, since they are able to celebrate the Divine office and administer the sacraments in their churches.[125] They are, therefore, obliged to make a profession of faith. Besides these rectors, the law also provides for rectors of public or semi-public oratories.[126] These, too, must make a profession of faith before they assume office, for certainly the care of souls is attached to their position as holders of a benefice.[127] Chaplains, i.e., priests who exercise a spiritual care over nuns, lay religious, confraternities, prisons, hospitals, and colleges, are seldom bound to make a profession of faith upon their appointment. The determining factor is whether or not their office is a juridical benefice and whether or not it has attached to it the care of souls.

[121] Cf. canon 451, § 3.

[122] Cf. *Facultates Castrenses,* issued by the Military Ordinariate of the United States to all army and navy chaplains in 1942.

[123] Cf. canon 1409.

[124] "Nomine rectorum ecclesiarum hic veniunt sacerdotes, quibus cura demandatur alicuius ecclesiae, quae nec paroecialis sit nec capitularis, nec adnexa domui communitatis religiosae, quae in eadem officia celebret."

[125] Cf. De Meester, *Compendium,* II, 356-358; Wernz-Vidal, *Ius Canonicum,* II, 897; Prümmer, *Manuale Iuris Canonici* (3. ed., Friburgi-Brisgoviae: Herder & Co., 1922), p. 225; Coronata, *Institutiones,* I, 600; canon 484, §§ 1, 2.

[126] Cf. canon 1188, § 2, 1°, 2°.

[127] Cf. Feldhaus, *Oratories* (The Catholic University of America Canon Law Studies, n. 42, Washington, D.C.: The Catholic University of America, 1927), pp. 96-108; Vermeersch-Creusen, *Epitome,* I, 388, n. 535; *AAS,* XI (1919), 340.

The obligation of profession of faith holds if the conditions are met.

In this country such benefices may have been set up in some institutions, particularly in those Catholic hospitals that have a residential chaplain who is appointed by the Ordinary. Although many of the state prisons have Catholic chaplains who receive a salary for their work as spiritual guides to the inmates, the office of prison chaplain is scarcely a true benefice, for it lacks the juridical elements that constitute a legal benefice, particularly foundation by competent ecclesiastical authority. While hospital chaplains appointed by the local Ordinary to that work, therefore, must often make a profession of faith, depending on whether or not their position is a true benefice, it does not seem likely that the priests to whom is committed the care of prisoners are bound by the obligation.

Although the Council of Trent gave those promoted to benefices a two months' period of grace before the penalties for non-compliance were enforced,[128] the present law is that profession of faith must be made either before taking office or in the act of assuming office.[129] It may be made to the Bishop in person, to the Vicar General, or to the delegate appointed by either of these, for the law prescribes that it be made before the local Ordinary, a term which, according to canon 198, § 2, includes both Bishop and Vicar General. It is the custom in many dioceses for those appointed to pastorates to make their profession of faith before the dean of their district, or before another pastor who has been delegated by the local Ordinary to receive the profession.

Article V. The Rector and the Professors of Theology, Canon Law, and Philosophy in Seminaries

Canon 1406.—§ 1. Obligatione emittendi professionem fidei . . . tenentur:

7°. Coram loci Ordinario eiusve delegato . . . rector, professores sacrae theologiae, iuris canonici, et philosophiae in Seminariis initio cuiuslibet anni scholastici vel saltem initio suscepti muneris;

The origin of the legislation that demands that rectors and professors of theology, philosophy, and canon law in seminaries make a

[128] Sess. XXIV, *de ref.*, cap. 12.

[129] Cf. *AAS*, III, 134.

profession of faith is the bull, *In sacrosancta,* issued by Pope Pius IV in 1564.[130] This document decreed that a profession of faith should be made by all teachers in Catholic schools, whether they were public or private.[131] As is evident, the present legislation is not so general. It demands that the rector,[132] the professors of theology, of canon law, and of philosophy make a profession of faith at the beginning of each scholastic year, or at least when they take over the duties of their office for the first time. From the wording of the canon, it seems that the wish of the Church is that the profession be taken each year, for only as a concession is it admitted that it need be taken only once, i. e., when the office is assumed. Ordinarily the Bishop is to judge whether the minimum requirement or the more desirable practice is to be followed.[133] Since the Code does not restrict the term "seminary," these provisions hold for all rectors and professors of the above-named disciplines, whether secular or religious, even exempt.[134] The provision of this canon would seem also to hold for the rectors of minor seminaries[135] and for the professors of philosophy, if that subject is taught in the minor seminary, for the terms, "seminary" and "philosophy," are not restricted in the canon. Theology and canon law, of course, are subjects that are strictly proper to a major seminary.

A pertinent question may here be raised: Does the obligation of making a profession of faith bind only the rector and the actual professors of theology, canon law, and philosophy, or does the obligation also extend to the professors in the various other subjects that are taught in the "departments" of theology, canon law, and philosophy?

The pre-Code legislation required that profession of faith be made by all teachers in Catholic schools, either private or public. The Holy See did not distinguish between teachers of the various arts and sciences, but demanded a profession from all, even those who taught such non-controversial subjects as mathematics and music.[136] The

[130] *Fontes,* n. 107.

[131] Cf. Wernz, *Ius Decretalium,* III, n. 14.

[132] Canon 1358: "Curandum ut in quolibet Seminario adsint rector pro disciplina, magistri pro instructione . . ."

[133] Cf. De Meester, *Compendium,* III, 318, nota 4.

[134] Cf. Blat, *Commentarium,* III, 425; Fanfani (*De Iure Religiosorum,* 2. ed., Taurini-Romae: Marietti, 1925, p. 137) declares that the obligation holds for professors in the convents of religious. This author errs, however, when he affirms that the profession of faith can be made before the religious superior.

[135] Cf. canon 1354, § 2.

[136] Cf. Chapter III, art. II, *supra.*

Code itself declares that the philosophical course must last at least two years and comprise, besides philosophy proper, also the allied branches,[137] which are officially described as follows: Mathematics, natural or physical science, literature, Latin, Greek, and history.[138] The present law declares that the theological course should comprise, besides dogmatic and moral theology, the study of Sacred Scripture, Church history, liturgy, sacred eloquence, ecclesiastical chant,[139] and pastoral theology.[140] Finally, the Code declares that at least Holy Scripture, dogmatic theology, moral theology, and Church history should be taught by distinct professors.[141]

In speaking of the seminary courses of philosophy, canon law, and theology, therefore, the law often seems to consider the general courses rather than the specific subjects that are included under those courses. But the canon under consideration does not make the distinction between general course and specific subject; it merely demands a profession of faith from the professors of theology, canon law, and philosophy. It would seem, therefore, that a profession is demanded only from the professors of these subjects and not from the teachers in the *departments* of the same name. This view is strengthened by the wording of canon 6, 6°, which declares that all disciplinary laws not contained either implicitly or explicitly in the Code have lost their force. It cannot be argued successfully that the pre-Code discipline is contained either implicitly or explicitly in the wording of the canon under consideration.[142]

It is to be noted that the Code demands the profession of faith to be made before the local Ordinary or his delegate. The persons designated by canon 198, § 2, therefore, are competent. The local Ordinary could well authorize the rector himself to receive the professions of the professors after or before the rector has made his profession to the Bishop, the Vicar General, or the delegate appointed by either. If the seminary is conducted by religious, the local Ordinary could delegate the religious superior to accept the professions.

137 Cf. canon 1365, § 1.

138 S. C. Consist., 12 iul. 1912, ad 9—*AAS,* IV, 496 et sq.; cf. Augustine, *A Commentary,* VI, 399.

139 Cf. canon 1365, § 2.

140 Cf. canon 1365, § 3.

141 Cf. canon 1366, § 3.

142 Blat (*Commentarium,* III, 425) seems to hold the opposite view, for he includes among those under obligation to make a profession of faith all in "disciplinis philosophicis, theologicis et iuridicis."

ARTICLE VI. SUBDEACONS

Canon 1406.—§ 1. Obligatione emittendi professionem fidei . . . tenentur:

7°. Coram loci Ordinario eiusve delegato . . . omnes promovendi ad ordinem subdiaconatus;

Under the common law before the promulgation of the Code it was held that all who were to be promoted to holy orders should make a profession of faith.[143] The law now releases from this obligation all those about to be ordained to minor or major orders except those who are to be promoted to the subdiaconate. It will be pointed out in another chapter, when the oath against Modernism is considered, that the Ordinary may also demand that a profession of faith be made by those about to be ordained deacons or priests.[144] But this is particular legislation and cannot be considered as obligatory by reason of the prescriptions of the Code. The latter merely demands that the profession of faith be made before the promotion to the subdiaconate. The manner usually employed is that the candidate makes the profession of faith at the same time that he takes the oath against Modernism and the oath that he freely accepts of his own free choice celibacy and the duties imposed by Holy Orders.

Either the local Ordinary or his delegate may receive the profession of faith from the subdeacons. The usual practice is that the rector of the seminary acts as delegate of the local Ordinary, but any cleric might be deputed for the function.

ARTICLE VII. CENSORS OF BOOKS

Canon 1406.—§ 1. Obligatione emittendi professionem fidei . . . tenentur:

7°. Coram loci Ordinario eiusve delegato . . . librorum censores, de quibus in can. 1393;

The obligation of the censors of books mentioned in canon 1393 to make a profession of faith is entirely new in the Code. The old law had no provision that they should make profession of faith. As a matter of fact, the legislation on censors that is contained in canon 1393 is largely taken from the *Motu proprio* of Pope Pius X, entitled

[143] Cf. c. 5, D. XXIII; Reiffenstuel, *Ius Canonicum*, I, 89.

[144] Cf. S. C. Consist., 24 martii 1911—*AAS*, III, 181 et sq.

Sacrorum Antistitum, and issued Sept. 1, 1910.[145] The rules therein enacted by the Sovereign Pontiff and repeated in canon 1393, § 1, are that every diocese must have *officially appointed* censors for the examination of writings that are to be published.[146]

It is to be noted that the canon demands that there be an *officially appointed* censor, i.e., one who regularly performs the duties of examining the books that are to be published. The presumption is that if one were chosen to be a censor in an emergency, to examine a book because the regularly appointed censor was unable to do so, he would not have to make a profession of faith, for he would not come under the classification of "censors of books mentioned in canon 1393."[147] The obligation of the Code in canon 1406, § 1, 7°, rests only on those who have been officially appointed for the examination of books. These should make their profession of faith upon taking office, and this profession suffices as long as their term of office lasts. There is no need for a repetition of the profession of faith whenever the office of censor is exercised, for the canon in question manifestly treats of the one profession of faith to be made when the regularly appointed censor of books takes over his office.

Since the term *local Ordinary* is again employed with reference to censors of books, those who have been appointed to the office of examining books may make their profession before the Bishop or his delegate or before the Vicar General or his delegate, who must be a cleric, or before any one of the others designated by law under the term, "local Ordinary."[148]

Article VIII. Confessors and Preachers

Canon 1406.—§ 1. Obligatione emittendi professionem fidei . . . tenentur:

7°. Coram loci Ordinario eiusve delegato . . . sacerdotes confessionibus excipiendis destinati et sacri concionatores, antequam facultate donentur ea munia exercendi;

[145] Cf. Augustine, *A Commentary,* VI, 451.

[146] "In universis Curiis episcopalibus censores ex officio adsint, qui edenda cognoscant."

[147] Augustine (*A Commentary,* VI, 451) brings out the distinction between the *ex officio* censors and the one appointed in an emergency, or to censor one book. He does not treat of the latter's obligation to make a profession of faith.

[148] Cf. canon 198, § 2.

The first regulation on profession of faith for confessors and preachers was promulgated in the IV Provincial Council of Milan.[149] This legislation was copied by many provinces, especially in Europe. Thus, a council held in Rome under Pope Benedict XIV in 1725 ruled that a profession of faith must be taken by preachers and confessors.[150] But this was particular legislation and did not bind the whole Church. The pre-Code universal discipline did not require a profession of faith from either confessors or preachers as such.

The canon under consideration speaks of "priests" who are to act as confessors or preachers. The only minister, of course, of the Sacrament of Penance is a priest.[151] But the Code itself provides that, besides priests, deacons may also be given the faculty to preach.[152] Are the latter, then, to be considered as bound by the obligation of making a profession of faith before the local Ordinary before they receive the faculty of preaching? Blat thinks so.[153] His contention is probably correct, for, since the purpose of this legislation is to prevent any heresy from being preached to the people, it follows that if the obligation binds priests who are given the faculty to preach, those who are less experienced than ordained priests, i.e., deacons, should also be required to confess the orthodox faith before they are allowed to preach. It cannot be successfully argued here that the Code wished specifically to limit the taking of the profession to priests by the use of the term, *"sacerdotes."* For, as has been noted, the purpose of the entire legislation on profession of faith is to prevent *any* person of doubtful faith from gaining positions in the exercise of which damage to the faith of the laity might be the result. Practically, there is little difficulty to be anticipated in the matter, particularly in the United States, for seldom, if ever, are deacons given the faculties for preaching.

Since the canon makes no distinction between secular or religious confessors and preachers, all without exception must make a profession of faith before they receive their faculties. The canon says, "before the local Ordinary or his delegate." What of the preacher brought

[149] Cf. Hardouin, X, 954.

[150] *Coll. Lac.*, I, 345-346; S.C.C. *in Comacelen.*, 24 aug. 1822—Pallottini, XV, 371-372, n. 37.

[151] Canon 871. "Minister huius sacramenti est solus sacerdos."

[152] Canon 1342, § 1. "Concionandi facultas solis sacerdotibus vel diaconis fiat . . ."

[153] *Commentarium,* III, 425.

in to speak to exempt religious or their dependents, according to the norm of canon 1338, § 1, and canon 514, § 1? Supposing he has not made the profession of faith before the local Ordinary by reason of other pulpit occupation in the diocese, does he now make it before the religious superior who, in terms of canon 1338, will grant him this faculty? It seems not, for canon 1406 does not list religious superiors as competent to receive the profession except in one instance, in canon 1406, § 1, 9°, when they appoint other superiors to office in the same exempt clerical religious organizations. Hence the preacher will have to be sent to the local Ordinary, or the superior in question may ask delegation to act for the Ordinary in receiving the profession of faith from the preacher.[154] The same is to be said of those who receive their faculties to hear Confessions from the superior of exempt clerical organizations, as provided in canon 875. They must make the required profession of faith before the local Ordinary and not before the religious superior.

There is little foundation to the argument that since the Code does not explicitly mention in canon 1406, § 1, 7°, members of exempt clerical institutions who get their faculties for preaching and hearing confessions from their religious superiors, these religious do not have to make a profession of faith before the local Ordinary.[155]

The canon under discussion is evidently meant to refer to all priests without exception, either secular or religious, even exempt. It would patently be wrong to affirm that the Code excepted religious in all canons in which the term "priest" is used and "religious priest" is not specifically mentioned. This is in effect the argument used by those who affirm that a profession of faith need not be taken by those religious who receive the faculties of preaching and hearing Confessions from their superiors.

The Holy See has solved some difficulties that have arisen regarding the profession of faith that must be taken by those who receive faculties for hearing Confessions and for preaching. It has ruled that if these faculties are given only for a year at a time there is no need to repeat the profession at the renewal of the faculties.[156] The probable reason for this decision is this: The Code speaks of first

[154] McVann (*The Canon Law on Sermon Preaching,* New York: Paulist Press, 1940, p. 163), supports this opinion.

[155] Cf. Woywod, "The Profession of Faith, "*Homiletic and Pastoral Review,* XXVIII, 1179-1183. Also holding this view are Blat (*Commentarium,* III, 425-426) and Fanfani (*De Iure Religiosorum,* p. 136).

[156] Cf. *AAS,* II, 856.

approval only, and the exercise of the faculties of preaching and hearing Confessions is not an office, but merely a duty sometimes attached to an office. The rule, therefore, of canon 1406, § 2, demanding that profession of faith be repeated by those appointed to a new office does not apply.[157]

The Sacred Consistorial Congregation has declared that if a person has made a profession of faith either for the faculty of hearing Confessions or preaching in one diocese, he need not repeat it when he seeks the faculties of another diocese.[158]

The two decisions that are quoted above form a solid argument that the profession of faith need not be repeated by those religious who receive the faculties from the local Ordinary in one diocese and then seek diocesan faculties from the local Ordinary of another diocese. Woywod may be correct in affirming that the latter could demand that the profession be repeated,[159] but the local Ordinary certainly cannot be considered as under obligation to do so, for the demands of the law would have been fulfilled by the profession the religious necessarily made before the local Ordinary when they received their first faculties.

Because the canon says that the profession of faith must be made before the local Ordinary or his delegate, the persons named in canon 198, § 2, are competent. This section specifically excludes religious superiors from the term, *local Ordinary*. It must be borne in mind, moreover, that if one were to seek the faculties for both preaching and hearing Confessions at the same time, the one and the same profession of faith would suffice.[160]

Article IX. Rectors and Faculties of Pontifical Universities

> *Canon 1406.—§ 1. Obligatione emittendi professionem fidei . . . tenentur:*
>
> *8°. Coram Ordinario eiusve delegato Rector Universitatis vel Facultatis; coram Rectore vero Universitatis vel Facultatis eiusve delegato, professores omnes in Universitate seu Facultate canonice erecta, initio cuiusque anni scholastici vel saltem initio suscepti muneris;*

[157] Cf. Woywod, *loc. cit.*

[158] S.C. Consist., 20 iunii 1913—*AAS,* V, 272;. cf. Vermeersch, *Periodica,* V, 210.

[159] *Loc. cit.*

[160] Cf. McVann, *The Canon Law on Sermon Preaching,* p. 163. The intrinsic reason will be discussed in Chap. VI, Art. I, *infra.*

The obligation of a rector of a university or faculty to make a profession of faith before the Ordinary or his delegate and of the professors to make their profession of faith before the rector derives directly from the constitution of Pope Pius IV, *In sacrosancta,* issued November 15, 1564.[161] The Code merely modifies the obligation of the professors to make it yearly, by allowing them to make the profession at the time they begin teaching.

The canon under discussion is evidently considering Catholic universities or faculties that have been canonically erected by the Holy See.[162] It does not apply to those professors, even priests, who have professorial chairs in secular universities, as is clear from a reply of Pope Pius X to one of the German Bishops on December 31, 1910.[163] To this further extent, then, has the law been changed, for the old legislation was directed to all universities and all faculties by Pope Pius IV.

The Code declares that the rector of a university or faculty must make his profession of faith before the Ordinary or his delegate, and it infers that the obligation binds only once, namely, when the rector assumes his duties at the university. Since the term "Ordinary" is here used, canon 198, § 1, is to be used in interpreting the meaning. This rules that besides the Roman Pontiff, residential Bishops in their territories, Abbots and Prelates *nullius,* and their Vicars General; Administrators, Vicars and Prefects Apostolic, and major superiors in clerical exempt religious institutes are also Ordinaries. Hence, if a Catholic university were in charge of a clerical exempt religious congregation, as is provided in the Code,[164] the rector might make the required profession of faith before his major religious superior and would not need to repeat it before the local Ordinary.[165] What is said here also applies to the presidents of Pontifical faculties, i.e., those established outside of canonically erected universities, as is evident from a decision of the Holy See in 1931.[166]

Although the pre-Code law demanded that the professors of universities or faculties make their profession of faith annually,[167] the

[161] Cf. *Fontes,* n. 107.

[162] Canon 1376, § 1. "Canonica constitutio catholicae studiorum Universitatis vel Facultatis Sedi Apostolicae reservatur."

[163] Cf. *AAS,* III, 19; Blat, *Commentarium,* III, 426.

[164] Cf. canon 1376, § 2.

[165] Blat (*Commentarium,* III, 426), upholds this opinion.

[166] Cf. S.C., Stud., *Ordinationes,* 12 iulii 1931—*AAS,* XXIII, 263.

[167] Cf. Wernz, *Ius Decretalium,* III, n. 14, ad VI.

present legislation makes it clear that if these professors make their profession before the rector or his delegate at the beginning of their teaching career, it is sufficient. But this is put forth as a minimum requirement. The Code would prefer that the profession be repeated at the beginning of each scholastic year. The command of the rector, the constitutions that have been approved by the Holy See, or local custom usually decides the practice to be followed in the particular universities.

Because of the vast growth of the educational system in the past two centuries, the development of new branches of learning, the desire of a greater number of the people to be truly educated, all universities, including those which have been canonically erected by the Holy See, have been forced to enlarge their curriculum and to add professors who are skilled in the various arts and sciences. This has meant, particularly for Catholic universities in countries where Catholics are in the minority, that often lay and even non-Catholic professors have been added to the staff. This fact brings to the fore a pertinent question: Is the canon under discussion meant to be interpreted as including all professors, even the non-Catholics? In deciding the question a knowledge of the meaning of the terms, "faculty" and "university," is necessary.

The pre-Code and classical definitions of university and faculty are these: A university includes a so-called general curriculum *(studium generale)*, or, in specific terms, the faculties of theology, philosophy, law, and medicine. The term, "faculty," on the other hand, in its restricted and technical sense means only one of these faculties. In the full sense of the term, a university means the total of the four faculties mentioned above.[168] The term, "faculty," was originally used in the more general sense of science or knowledge; later it became some department of study. In its present full sense, it means any of the courses mentioned above that is taught in a university.[169] Whether this acceptance of the terms was in the minds of the compilers of the Code when they wrote canon 1376 and canon 1406, § 1, 8°, cannot be determined. Pre-Code authors are mainly concerned with the conflict of authorities, civil and ecclesiastical, in the government of universities.[170] The result is that they do not consider

[168] Cf. Pace, Edward, "Universities"—*The Catholic Encyclopedia,* XV, 188-198; Coronata, *Institutiones,* II, 308; Wernz, *Ius Decretalium,* III, n. 83-89.

[169] Cf. Augustine, *A Commentary,* VI, 420.

[170] Cf. Wernz, *loc. cit.*

the case of an ecclesiastical or Catholic university in which courses other than the classical subjects of theology, philosophy, law, and medicine are treated.

The problem that arises in a consideration of the present canon, however, does not concern itself with the question whether or not "university" and "faculty" are to be taken in their restricted sense or are meant to designate a faculty outside the four classical ones. Even in one of the latter there might be non-Catholic members. Under the course of philosophy, for example, is included the so-called experimental psychology, which has as authorities many non-Catholics. It is by no means inconceivable that one of these authorities would teach his subject in a Catholic university. In like manner, in the subjects of civil law and medicine many non-Catholics might be employed by a Catholic university, particularly in regions where there is a scarcity of Catholic professional men. Do these non-Catholic members of a Catholic university's faculty have the obligation of making a profession of faith under the regulations of canon 1406, § 1, 8°? The question might also be asked: Do non-Catholic professors of subjects not included in the four classical courses have to make a profession of faith? In order to settle the second question first, it is the author's opinion that such professors are not included under canon 1406, § 1, 8°. The reason is this: The Church has not contemplated in her modern legislation the inclusion of all the faculties in a Pontifically erected university. If such were the case, the director of physical education, would be called on to make a profession of faith, which is a *reductio ad absurdum.* It must be remembered that the whole tenor of the legislation on profession of faith contemplates the safeguarding of the faith of the faithful by demanding such profession from clerical leaders and teachers. Certainly a teacher of mathematics is in no position to teach heresy or undermine the faith of his students.

There is a difficulty, however, with regard to those non-Catholic professors who are faculty members in one of the four classical courses. If they are not baptized, the question is easily solved. Canon 12 rules that laws that are purely ecclesiastical in their nature do not bind unbaptized persons.[171] The law that demands a profession of faith from faculty members is purely ecclesiastical in nature. Unbaptized faculty members are, therefore, not included in the obligation, although a question might be raised as to the obligation of a university of not employing such teachers. But what of those who are baptized and are heretics or schismatics?

[171] "Legibus mere ecclesiasticis non tenentur qui baptismum non receperunt. . ."

By Baptism a person becomes a subject of the Church and has all the rights and duties of a Christian, unless, insofar as rights are concerned, there is some obstacle impeding the bond of communion with the Church.[172] It seems to be the intention of the Church to oblige baptized non-Catholics to observe at least those laws that concern the common good and safeguard the public order.[173] Cicognani says:

> The same holds true with regard to inhabilitating laws and the general laws on delicts and penalties, or enactments pertaining to human acts, as, for example, in the matter of contracts, the juridical effects of fear or ignorance. If they were born and reared in the Church, or after their conversion left the Church, they are bound also to the observance of laws that concern their own sanctification. On the other hand, if they were born and reared in heresy or schism, apparenlty they are not held to such laws, for example, those regarding holydays, fast and abstinence.[174]

But many others, including Van Hove,[175] Coronata,[176] and Augustine [177] hold that baptized non-Catholics are bound by all ecclesiastical laws from which they are not specifically exempt. Thus, there is a probable opinion on both sides.[178] But even if the less strict opinion is followed, it is difficult to excuse non-Catholic professors from making the profession of faith on the grounds that such an act is one of personal sanctification. Rather would it be one of public good.

[172] Cf. canon 87.

[173] Cf. Vermeersch-Creusen, *Epitome,* 1, 104.

[174] *Canon Law,* 566. The same author has this also to say: "This opinion is regarded as probable by several authors; hence in practice it may be held as certain, but they consider these heretics and schismatics excused from sin because of their ignorance of the law."—*Ibid.* Cf. Vermeersch-Creusen, *loc. cit.*

[175] *De Legibus Ecclesiasticis,* p. 201: "Etinim lex fertur quoque pro illis qui probabiliter eam non servabunt, nec obligatio servandi legem est apud haereticos in damnum animarum, cum plerique vel bona fide vel ignorantia a peccato formali excusentur."

[176] *Institutiones,* I, 27: ". . . quare nullo solido fundamento canonico nititur distinctio ab aliquibus fieri solita circa leges bonum publicum aut bonum privatum respicientes, excusando ab his haereticos et schismaticos in bona fide educatos."

[177] *A Commentary,* I, 88.

[178] Cf. Van Hove, *op. cit.,* p. 202.

Practically, the only excuse for non-Catholics in this matter is the fact that the Church refuses to force anyone to perform an act contrary to his conscience. Now, profession of faith in the dogmas of the Catholic Church would certainly be an act against the conscience of a convinced heretic or schismatic. Even if they were indifferent members of their sect, profession of faith in the Catholic doctrine would be a meaningless ceremony to them. An indication of the Church's mind on the matter is to be found in the Statutes of the Catholic University of America, where it is specifically stated that non-Catholic professors are not bound to make a profession of faith. These statutes were approved by the Holy See.[179] In the absence of such a ruling from the Holy See, however, it would seem that a canonically erected Pontifical university would sin at least against the spirit of the law on profession of faith by employing a non-Catholic professor, at least in any of the four classical courses.

Article X. Those Awarded Academic Degrees

Canon 1406.—§ 1. Obligatione emittendi professionem fidei . . . tenentur:

8° . . . coram Rectore . . . eiusve delegato . . . itemque qui, periculo facto, academicis gradibus donanur;

The legislation demanding that a profession of faith be made by those who have passed the required examination before they receive academic degrees is not new with the Code. It has been pointed out in a previous chapter of this work that this regulation was embodied in the constitution, *In sacrosancta,* of Pope Pius IV.[180] The only change made in the Code is that the profession must be made before the rector or his delegate. The old law ruled that it must be made before the Bishop or his Vicar.[181]

The academic degrees here spoken of are those granted in Pontifical universities or faculties in the courses of theology, philosophy, and law. Since the Code does not specify, all the academic grades must be considered, namely the doctorate, the licentiate, and the baccalaureate. Augustine denies that the latter is, strictly speaking, an academic degree. He affirms that it is to be regarded "only as a

[179] Cf. *Statutes of the Catholic University of America* (Washington, D. C., 1927), Art. 50.

[180] Cf. *Fontes,* n. 107; *supra,* p. 40.

[181] Cf. Reiffenstuel, *Ius Canonicum,* I, 90.

stepping-stone" to other degrees.[182] But this opinion seems to be erroneous in the light of Papal pronouncements on the matter. Pope Leo XII in 1824 declared that those who receive the baccalaureate must make a profession of faith.[183] Pius XI in his encyclical, *Deus scientiarum Dominus,* dated May 24, 1931, declared that the baccalaureate is an academic degree.[184] The same Pontiff also specifically mentioned the profession of faith that must be taken by those who receive the baccalaureate in Sacred Scripture.[185]

The time of the profession is indicated in the canon itself, namely after the candidates for degrees have successfully passed their examinations and before their respective degrees are officially conferred. Augustine declares: "The profession may most properly be made in the chapel or church, before the staff, board, or faculty of the university, and in the presence of the students, or in the *aula academica* before the rector and some of the professors."[186] This, however, is merely a suggestion. The Code only demands that a profession of faith be made before the rector or his delegate. This regulation could easily be followed by requiring all those who are to receive degrees to make their profession before the dean of their respective schools, or to some other priest who has been deputed for this office. The profession can take place in any appropriate place—chapel, class room, or assembly hall.

Article XI. Superiors of Clerical Institutes

Canon 1406.—§ 1. Obligatione emittendi professionem fidei . . . tenentur:

9°. Coram Capitulo vel Superiore qui eos nominavit eorumve delegato, Superiores in religionibus clericalibus.

Although Pope Pius IV ruled that every religious prelate was required to make a profession of faith,[187] the pre-Code law was not

182 Cf. *A Commentary,* VI, 489.

183 Cf. *Bullarii Romani Continuatio Summorum Pontificum,* XIII, 167.

184 "Baccalaureatus est gradus academicus ex quo cognoscitur eum qui hoc gradu donatur tale suae doctrinae specimen dedisse, ut idoneus censeatur ad curriculum persequendum pro gradibus academicis superioribus."—*AAS,* XXIII, 241-262, Art. 8, "Normae Generales."

185 Encyclical, *Bibliorum scientiam,* 27 aprilis 1924—*AAS,* XVI, 180.

186 *A Commentary,* VI, 489.

187 Const., *Iniunctum nobis,* 13 nov. 1564, ad 1—*Fontes,* n. 108.

clear in demanding that superiors of clerical institutes should make a profession of faith, nor that it be made before the chapter or the superior who elected them. Now the Code does demand it of superiors of the above-mentioned clerical institutes, i.e., the majority of whose members are destined for the priesthood.[188]

The present law distinguishes between those who are *superiors,* e.g., of a religious house of a clerical organization, and those who are *major superiors,* who are as follows:

> The Abbot Primate, i.e., the Abbot of St. Anselm's in Rome; the abbot superior of a monastic congregation, the abbot of an independent monastery, even though it forms a part of the monastic congregation; the superior-general of the whole institute, the provincial superior, their vicars, and all others who have powers equivalent to those of provincials.[189]

Among the major superiors should also be included the vicar general of an institute, the visitors of men religious, and the vice-provincial. In many institutes, moreover, the first assistant or the first counsellor of the superior-general exercises supreme authority when the general is absent or impeded. When this first assistant or counsellor actually takes the place of the superior-general he has the powers of a major superior, but he can scarcely be called a major superior.[190]

Among the major superiors that have been mentioned, all save the provincials, their vicars, and others who have power equivalent to that of provincials, i.e., the vicars general and the vice provincials, are elected by a chapter.[191] Provincials, etc., are appointed by a higher superior after consultation with, or the consent of, his council.[192]

Besides the major superiors are those who are called *minor superiors.*[193] These are the superiors of religious houses, monasteries, friaries; novice masters, etc. They are always appointed by a religious superior.

In light of this explanation, then, by reason of the legislation of canon 1406, § 1, 9°, the Abbot Primate, the abbot superior of a

[188] Cf. canon 488, 4; Creusen-Garesche-Ellis, *Religious Men and Women in the Code* (Milwaukee: Bruce, 1940), p. 10.

[189] Cf. canon 488, 8.

[190] Cf. Creusen-Garesche-Ellis, *op. cit.,* pp. 16, 17.

[191] Creusen-Garesche-Ellis, *op. cit.,* p. 50; canons 506, 507.

[192] Creusen-Garesche-Ellis, *loc. cit.*

[193] Fanfani, *De Iure Religiosorum,* p. 56.

monastic congregation, the abbot of an independent monastery, and the superior general of a religious institute must make a profession of faith before the chapter that elected them, provided their institute is clerical. All other superiors, both major and minor, of clerical religious institutes, must make their profession of faith before the religious superior who appointed them, or his delegate. Both those who are required to make a profession of faith before a chapter and those who must make it before their religious superiors should fufilll that obligation. That they should make a profession of faith before or in the very act of taking office follows from the tenor of the whole legislation on the matter. It is the evident mind of the legislator that profession of faith be made before or in the act of taking office as an indication of the doctrinal soundness of the one promoted.

It is to be noted that the canon requires the profession only from clerical religious superiors. Heads of lay institutes, therefore, even though they are priests, are not bound by the obligation.[194] The obligation does bind, however, all clerical religious superiors, even those of exempt institutes. The canon makes no distinction when demanding the profession of faith between religious who are exempt from the jurisdiction of the local Ordinary and those subject to his jurisdiction. The Code Commisison, moreover, has declared that superiors of clerical societies without vows are bound to make a profession of faith according to the norms of canon 1406, § 1, 9°.[195]

It is to be noted that the particular constitutions of the various institutes are to be followed in the manner of elections or appointments. Where the constitutions call for an election of a local superior rather than his appointment by a higher superior, the one nominated must make his profession before the chapter that has elected him, even though he is technically only a minor superior.[196]

[194] Fanfani, *op. cit.*, p. 136.

[195] *CIC*, 25 iulii 1925—*AAS*, XVIII, 393.

[196] The Dominican constitutions provide that a prior is elected by the chapter of each priory.

CHAPTER VI

RENEWAL OF PROFESSION OF FAITH AND THE VALUE OF CUSTOM IN THE OBLIGATION OF MAKING THE PROFESSION

ARTICLE I. RENEWAL OF PROFESSION OF FAITH

Canon 1406.—§ 2. Qui, priore dimisso, aliud officium vel beneficium aut dignitatem etiam eiusdem speciei consequuntur, rursus debent fidei professionem emittere ad normam huius canonis.

In previous chapters of this work there has been made passing mention of the obligation of renewing profession of faith in certain instances. The specific obligation of renewal will now be considered. The history of renewal of profession of faith when one who had already made it received a new benefice or dignity dates far back into pre-Code legislation.[1] The present law demands that profession of faith be repeated according to the rules prescribed in the first paragraph of canon 1406 whenever one assumes a new office, benefice, or dignity, even if the new office is of the same species as the old. Thus, if a canon or dignitary of a cathedral church obtains a new dignity in the chapter, he must renew his profession of faith.[2] If one would lose any office, benefice, or dignity in any manner, e.g., by official removal, dismissal, resignation, etc., he would have to make another profession of faith upon his appointment to another benefice, office, or dignity.[3] It must be remembered that the canon demands the renewal of profession of faith after loss of office for any reason, not merely resignation. Hence, if a person were removed from office for refusal to obey his superiors, for a crime to which is attached the canonical penalty of removal from office,[4] or for any other reason, even though the removal lasted only for a short period, he would have to renew his profession of faith upon being appointed to the same or another benefice or office.[5]

[1] Cf. S.C.C., *in Terasonen.*, 20 aprilis 1782—*Thesaurus*, LI, 55; also S.C.C., *in Usseullen.*, 1 sept. 1759—*Thesaurus*, XXIII, 94; S.C.C., *in Dubia*, 1 aprilis 1786—Pallottini, XV, 396, n. 16.

[2] Cf. Augustine, *A Commentary*, VI, 489-490.

[3] Cf. Blat, *Commentarium*, III, 427.

[4] Cf. canons 2147-2156.

[5] Cf. De Meester, *Compendium*, III, 318, nota 7.

The same holds true of the person who has one benefice, office, or dignity and is appointed to another that is compatible with the keeping of his first position, e.g., a pastor who is appointed a diocesan consultor. Such a person would have to make a new profession of faith before or when he took up his new position. In like manner, if one were appointed to another position of the same kind, e.g., if a religious superior were transferred from one house to another, keeping the same rank, he would have to reiterate the profession of faith.[6]

It is possible that a cleric would be appointed simultaneously to several offices to which is annexed the obligation of making a profession of faith. Is one profession sufficient for all offices in this event, or is the profession to be repeated for each office or benefice? According to a declaration of the Sacred Consistorial Congregation, the obligation can be satisfied by one and the same profession of faith if the person before whom the profession of faith must be made is the same person, e.g., the local Ordinary.[7] If the persons to whom the profession of faith must be made are distinct, e.g., the religious chapter and the local Ordinary in the case of one who is at the same time nominated a religious superior and appointed a pastor of a parish,[8] two professions of faith must be made by that person. The reason for the decision of the Holy See may be found in the principle that many ecclesiastical precepts concerning the same thing may be fulfilled with one act. For example, it is sufficient to fulfill the precept of hearing Mass on a holy day of obligation that happens to fall on a Sunday by attending the Divine Sacrifice only once.

Article II. Custom

Canon 1408.—Reprobatur quaelibet consuetudo contra canones huius tituli.

There can be no doubt that before the promulgation of the Code customs contrary to the prescriptions of the law demanding that profssion of faith be made really existed.[9] Such customs are abrogated

[6] Cf. Blat, *Commentarium,* III, 427.

[7] S.C. Consist., 25 oct. 1910—*AAS,* II, 856; cf. Coronata, *Institutiones,* II, 352; Blat, *loc. cit.,* Vermeersch, *Periodica,* V, 232.

[8] Cf. canon 1406, § 1, 7, et 9.

[9] The Bishop of an Argentine diocese revealed in a request to the Sacred Congregation of the Council late in the last century that it had been the custom in his diocese for removable pastors not to make a profession of

by canon 5, which rules that customs, whether universal or particular, which were in vogue contrary to the prescriptions of the new law when the Code was promulgated, if they are expressly abrogated in the canons, should be amended as corruptions of the law, even though they were immemorial.

What is to be said of customs against making a profession of faith according to the norms of canon 1406 which may now be in existence? [10] The Code does provide that a community which is capable of receiving ecclesiastical law is able to introduce a custom that has the force of law, provided the consent of the proper ecclesiastical superior is obtained.[11] The Code also provides that in order that a custom may have the power to change an ecclesiastical law, it must be reasonable and lawfully prescribed by a continuous and uninterrupted usage of forty years.[12] But it also expressly states that any custom that is expressly reprobated in the law of the Code is not reasonable,[13] and since there is such an express reprobation in canon 1408, any custom that already exists, or had existed, i.e., whether present or past, is abrogated, and future custom is made impossible against the law of making profession of faith.[14]

faith (a violation of pre-Code legislation); that even those who were appointed to irremovable benefices did not make their profession of faith to the Bishop or his Vicar, but only to a priest who had been delegated by the Bishop to receive such professions.—S.C.C., 9 martii 1892—*Acta Sanctae Sedis* (Romae, 1865-1908), XXIV, 676, 677. Hereafter cited *ASS*.

[10] Despite the clear regulations of the Code demanding a profession of faith, the practice of not making the profession is all too widely followed, especially by those who are appointed to benefices to which is attached the care of souls. Less than ten years ago a New Zealand priest, writing of the profession of faith demanded of pastors, revealed that many in his diocese did not make the required profession when they took over their parishes; that profession of faith was usually made by these pastors at the next annual synod at which they attended; that at the synods the names of those who should make a profession were often forgotten.—"Profession of Faith Before Taking Possession of a Parish," *Australasian Catholic Record* (Manly, N.S.W., 1923—), X (1933), p. 147.

[11] Canon 26. "Communitas quae legis ecclesiasticae saltem recipiendae capax est, potest consuetudinem inducere quae vim legis obtineat."

Canon 25. "Consuetudo in Ecclesia vim legis a consensu competentis superioris Ecclesiastici unice obtinet."

[12] Canon 27, § 1. "Sed neque iuri ecclesiastico praeiudicium affert, nisi fuerit rationabilis et legitime per annos quadraginta continuos et completos praescripta . . ."

[13] Canon 27, § 2. "Consuetudo quae in iure expresse reprobatur, non est rationabilis."

[14] Cf. Augustine, *A Commentary*, VI, 490, 382.

This abrogation of contrary custom does not prevent a custom regarding profession of faith that is outside of the law *(praeter legem)*, i.e., one that has been knowingly introduced by a community with the intention of binding itself. Such a custom, provided it is reasonable and legitimately prescribed, obtains the force of law if it is observed for fully forty successive years.[15] Thus, a Bishop could permit the custom by which all priests in his diocese would make a profession of faith upon their appointment, even assistants and priests engaged in such work as the Catholic press, Catholic education, etc. If the priests bound themselves willingly to such a practice for forty successive years, the custom would have the force of law and would have to be followed by all the priests of the diocese thenceforth.

[15] Cf. canon 28; Cicognani, *Canon Law*, p. 658.

CHAPTER VII

PENALTIES FOR NEGLECT OF THE PROFESSION OF FAITH

Canon 2403.—Qui contra praescriptum can. 1406 fidei professionem sine iusto impedimento emittere negligat, moneatur, praefinito quoque congruo termino; quo transacto, contumax, etiam per privationem officii, beneficii, dignitatis, muneris, puniatur; nec interim beneficii, officii, dignitatis, muneris fructus facit suos.

The Council of Trent provided that if a person who had been appointed to a benefice to which was attached the care of souls or a person who had been appointed to a canonry or dignity in a Cathedral chapter did not make a profession of faith within two months after taking possession of his office, the revenues of the office were to be forfeited and the possession of the office or dignity was not to be recognized as canonical.[1] He was obliged to make restitution of the fruits of his benefice, even before sentence was pronounced by an ecclesiastical judge.[2] The censure of excommunication *(latae sententiae)* imposed in the constitution, *In sacrosancta,* by Pope Pius IV on superiors who retained their positions as teachers without making a profession of faith [3] was abrogated, according to Wernz, by the constitution, *Apostolicae Sedis,* of Pope Pius IX.[4] That this author is correct in this assertion is without doubt true, for the Pontiff specifically stated that all censures that were not mentioned in *Apostolicae Sedis* were abrogated.[5] It is a matter of fact that the censure in question is not contained in the constitution.

[1] Sess. XXIV *de ref.,* cap. 12.

[2] Wernz (*Ius Decretalium,* III, n. 20) points out that some theologians held that restitution was not obligatory before the sentence had been pronounced. But, he affirms, this opinion cannot be held as probable. His argument is as follows: "Etenim lex Tridentina non tantum est personalis, sed etiam conditionalis, i.e., fructus ab Ecclesia beneficiato tantum conceduntur sub conditione impleta de fidei professione. Hinc deficiente conditione fructus percepti sunt alieni, sed res aliena ante iudicis sententiam restitui debet. Quae restitutio fiat necesse est fabricae ecclesiae, si illa indiget vel alteri pio loco vel pauperibus praesertim loci pro arbitrio Ordinarii loci, nisi condonatio fructuum illegitime perceptorum obtineatur."

[3] Cf. *Fontes,* n. 107.

[4] Cf. *Fontes,* n. 21.

[5] ". . . re diu ac matura perpenso, motu proprio, certa scientia, matura deliberatione Nostra, deque Apostolicae Nostrae potestatis plenitudine, hac

But the declaration contained in the constitution of Pope Pius IV that those who received academic grades, at least in theology and canon law, without a profession of faith did not have true canonical degrees still held before the Code was promulgated.[6]

A penal law that ceased to be effective after 1918 was that which demanded that Bishops who refused to make a profession of faith in the provincial council were to be reported to Rome and the other Bishops were to abstain from communion with them. The old legislation that those in possession of benefices who did not make a profession of faith in the first diocesan synod after their appointment should be punished by the Bishop according to the norms of the sacred canons also lost effect after the Code's promulgation.[7]

Article I. Minor Penalties

There is no doubt that the Code in canon 2403 has introduced a new disciplinary legislation for those who are remiss in fulfilling their obligation of making a profession of faith.[8] The pre-Code penalties must, therefore, according to the principles of canon 6, 5, be considered abrogated.[9]

The present law indicates that, though the obligation of fulfilling the precept of profession of faith is grave indeed,[10] and urges until the obligation is fulfilled,[11] the fact of non-fulfillment does not in itself constitute a bar to the valid possession of the offices which demand a profession of faith from the incumbent. A pastor, for

perpetuo valitura Constitutione decernuimus, et ex quibuscumque censuris sive excommunicationis, sive suspensionis, sive interdicti, quae per modum latae sententiae, ipsoque facto incurrendae, hactenus impositae sunt, non nisi illae quae in hac ipsa Constitutione inserimus . . ."—*Fontes,* n. 552.

[6] Cf. Wernz, *loc. cit.*

[7] Cf. Sess. XXIV *de ref.*, cap. 12; Wernz, *loc. cit.*

[8] D'Angelo, "De Professione Fidei," *Apollinaris* (Romae, 1928—), I, 415-417.

[9] "Quod ad poenas attinet, quarum in Codice nulla fit mentio, spirituales sint vel temporales, medicinales vel ut vocant, vindicativae, latae vel ferendae sententiae, eae tanquam abrogatae habeantur."

[10] Cf. Coronata, *Institutiones,* II, 351.

[11] Cf. De Meester, *Compendium,* III, 317; Cocchi, *Commentarium in Codicem Iuris Canonici* (VI, *De Rebus,* Taurini-Romae: Marietti, 1924), VI, 179.

example, who assumed his position without making the required profession of faith is validly in possession of his benefice and can exercise all of the duties thereof until such time as he is deprived of his position because of the failure. If action against his neglect is not takn by his competent superior, he remains in valid possession of his office until his removal, resignation, or transfer because of death or some other cause. This valid possession prescinds, of course, from the morality of such an action. If a pastor were cognizant of his obligation of making a profession of faith as prescribed by canon 1406, he would sin gravely if he were to neglect it.

What has been said of the obligation of pastors in the foregoing holds equally well for the obligation of all others who are bound to profession by reason of canon 1406, for canon 2403 admits of no exceptions to the rule.

The penalty imposed by the present law on those who are negligent in making a profession of faith is *ferendae sententiae* [12] in so far as the privation of office, benefice, or dignity, or some less severe penalty, is imposed on the one who has been warned to make a profession of faith and stubbornly refuses to do so. It is *latae sententiae* in so far as it takes away the revenue of the culprit's benefice, office, or dignity from the time he refuses to comply with the demand that he fulfill his obligation and make the profession of faith.[13]

But there are certain conditions that must be verified before either penalty can be incurred. Canon 2403 speaks of the person who neglects to make a profession of faith according to the precept of canon 1406 without a *just* or *legitimate* impediment. This is to say that the impediment must be proportionate to the law in seriousness. Since the law binds *sub gravi,* there must be a serious reason for the non-fulfillment of the precept.[14]

If a pastor was too ill to make a profession of faith at the time of his appointment, there would exist for him a legitimate impediment. If it was impossible, moreover, for the pastor to make a

[12] Canon 2217, § 1. "Poena dicitur: 2°. . . . *ferendae sententiae,* si a iudice vel Superiore infligi debeat."

[13] Canon 2217, § 1. "Poena dicitur: 22°. *Latae sententiae,* si poena determinata ita sit addita legi vel praecepto ut incurratur ipso facto commissi delicti;" cf. Chelodi, *Ius Poenale* (4. ed., Tridenti: Libreria Moderna Editrice, A. Ardesi, 1935), pp. 150-151; D'Angelo, "De Professione Fidei," *Apollinaris, loc. cit.;* Blat, *Commentarium* (V, *De Delictis et Poenis,* Romae: Collegio "Angelico," 1924), V, 313.

[14] Cf. Blat, *loc. cit.*

profession before the local Ordinary or his delegate because of long distances, inclement weather, etc., the penalty could not be imposed because such circumstances must also be considered as just impediments.

It should be noted that the Code in prescribing the penalty for the non-fulfillment of the precept of canon 1406 uses the word, "neglect" *(negligat)*. This implies a full cognizance of the obligation and an adequate time to ocmply with it. One who forgets to fulfill an obligation, one who has no available time between the notification of appointment and his installation, and at the time of installation itself, to make a profession of faith, or one who is unaware of his obligation cannot be said to *neglect* making a profession of faith.[15]

According to present legislation, the first step in the carrying out of the ecclesiastical penalty against those who neglect the obligation of profession of faith is the canonical admonition. It is a principle of law that the penalties cannot be ordinarily inflicted[16] unless the delinquent has first been rebuked and admonished to recede from his contumacy and such time for repentance has been given him as the judge or superior deems proper in the particular case.[17] It does not seem necessary, however, that this admonition be given in a strictly judicial manner.[18]

The purpose of this admonition in the case of the one negligent in the matter of profession of faith is to force him to make it. The Code does not strictly say that the admonition is made to force the profession, but the context of canon 2403 implies this.[19] The admonition is to be made by the superior who is competent to inflict the consequent penalty if the admonition is not heeded.[20] With regard to pastors, canons, Vicars General, and others mentioned in canon 1406, § 1, 5°, 6°, 7°, et 8°, the competent superior for the imposing of

[15] Cf. Blat, *loc. cit.*

[16] Under certain circumstances, penalties other than censures may be inflicted without previous warning, e.g., as provided for in canon 2222. Cf. Woywod, *A Practical Commentary,* II, 423-424.

[17] Canon 2233, § 2. "Licet id legitime constet, si agatur de infligenda censura, reus reprehendatur ac moneatur ut a contumacia recedat ad normam can. 2242, § 3, dato, si prudenti eiusdem iudicis vel Superioris arbitrio casus id ferat, congruo ad resipiscentiam tempore . . ."

[18] Cf. Coronata, *Institutiones,* IV, 653.

[19] Cf. Coronata, *Institutiones,* IV, 652.

[20] Cf. Blat, *Commentarium,* V, 313.

the penalty is the Ordinary,[21] but not the Vicar General, for the latter cannot inflict penalties without a special mandate.[22] The time that must be given by the superior for the fulfilling of the command to make a profession of faith is not stated by the canon, but certainly a reasonable period of time is meant. This would range from two weeks to a month, depending on the circumstances of the case, e.g., distance from the parish to the Episcopal city, difficulties of transportation, and the like.[23]

If the time given to the person who has not made his profession of faith has elapsed without his fulfilling the obligation, he is to be considered contumacious [24] and the competent superior is to proceed to inflict the penalties of law on him. According to canon 2403, the penalty is indeterminate as to its minimum, determined as to its maximum, i.e., deprivation of office, benefits, etc.[25] A Bishop, therefore, could punish a pastor who was recalcitrant in the matter of profession of faith with suspension from the acts of the power of orders for a specified time,[26] a fine of a month's salary, or any other discipline that would, in his judgment, be a fitting penalty.

Article II. Deprivation of Office

It must be understood that the punishment inflicted by the Ordinary on those who refuse to make a profession of faith after being admonished to do so cannot be more stringent than deprivation of office, for the Code specifically states that deprivation of office is the maximum penalty. This is indicated by the use of the words, "even by" *(etiam per)*.

Thus, excommunication, perpetual suspension, deposition, perpetual deprivation of the ecclesiastical garb, or degradation [27] could not be imposed as punishments upon those who neglect to make a pro-

[21] Cf. canon 198, § 1.

[22] Canon 2220, § 2. "Vicarius Generalis sine mandato speciali non habet potestatem infligendi poenae."

[23] Cf. Coronata, *loc. cit.*

[24] Canon 2242, § 2. "Si agatur de censuris ferendae sententiae contumax est qui, non obstantibus monitionibus . . . a delicto non desistit . . ."

[25] Cf. D'Angelo, *loc. cit.*

[26] Cf. canon 2279, § 1.

[27] Cf. canon 2298.

fession of faith. It is possible, however, that the one who refuses to comply with the obligation of profession of faith after being admonished to do so by his competent superior would be what the Code calls "suspect of heresy." If one suspect of heresy does not amend within six months after the penalties have been imposed, he is to be considered a heretic and is liable to the penalties for heresy,[28] which are excommunication, deprivation of benefice or other position the guilty person may have in the Church, infamy by disposition of law, and deposition.[29]

Article III. Deprivation of Revenues

To the sanction *ferendae sententiae* that is imposed by law on those neglecting to make a profession of faith after being admonished to do so, there is another which is *latae sententiae,* incurred at the time the offense is committed. This latter penalty provides that the offender cannot make use of the revenue of his office. It is as it were a penalty by virtue of which if the person subject to this punishment would ask for these revenues, he would be demanding something not his own.[30] If the guilty party did receive these revenues, the Ordinary would not be able to condone the act, and restitution would be necessary even without a declaratory sentence.[31] The law does not provide what is to be done with the revenues that are forfeited by the delinquent person, as it does in the case of a pastor who is illegitimately absent from his parish,[32] so the use of the revenues is left to the prudent judgment and conscience of the Ordinary. Usually they should be turned back to the parish, the benefice, or the office occupied by the guilty person.[33]

There is some discussion among canonists about the time at which the *latae sententiae* penalty begins to be effective. Are the revenues belonging to the one who refuses to make a profession of faith to be computed from the date on which he assumed his position, the date

[28] Cf. canon 2315.

[29] Cf. canon 2314, § 1.

[30] Cf. D'Angelo, *loc. cit.*

[31] Cf. Augustine, *A Commentary* (VIII, 3. ed., St. Louis: Herder, 1931), VIII, 504; Coronata, *Institutiones,* IV, 653; D'Angelo, *loc. cit.*

[32] Canon 2381, 1, provides that the Ordinary shall distribute these revenues to the church itself, to some pious place, or to the poor.

[33] Cf. D'Angelo, *loc. cit.*

on which he received the canonical admonition, or the date on which he became contumacious? The answer to this question is to be found in the interpretation of the word, "*interim,*" used in the canon. Some canonists hold that the word means the whole time in which there was negligence in making the profession of faith.[34] Their reasoning may be summed up as follows: The reason for the penalty is the fault, and a beneficiary is at fault when he neglects his duty. Now the beginning of negligence dates from the time when a person who is able to and must make a profession of faith does not fulfill this obligation, i.e., when he assumes his office. Therefore all the revenues of the negligent person from the time he assumed his office are forfeited.[35]

The better opinion seems to be that which holds that only those revenues that accrue after the person has become contumacious are forfeited.[36] This opinion holds that the reason for the penalty is not the fault, but the contumacy after the warning has been given. Its proponents hold that the *latae sententiae* punishment begins at the very moment there is contumacy, not before. Only those revenues, therefore, which are received after the negligent person becomes contumacious are forfeited.

The wording of canon 2403 seems to favor this opinion, for the clause introduced by the word, "*interim,*" must be regarded, according to the rules of rhetoric, as modifying the second rather than the first clause of the sentence.

What has been affirmed here of the penalties for neglect of profession of faith does not apply to neglect of the anti-Modernist oath.[37] Those who are remiss in their obligation of taking the anti-Modernist oath are to be reported to the Holy Office by their superiors.[38]

[34] Cf. Eichmann, *Das Strafrecht des Codex Iuris Canonici* (Paderborn: Schoningh, 1920), p. 231; Chelodi, *Ius Poenale,* p. 151.

[35] Cf. D'Angelo, *loc. cit.;* Eichmann, *loc. cit.*

[36] Cf. Coronata, *Institutiones,* IV, 653; Augustine, *A Commentary,* VIII, 504.

[37] Cf. Vermeersch-Creusen, *Epitome,* III, 376.

[38] Cf. *Fontes,* n. 689, ad VII.

CHAPTER VIII

THE ANTI-MODERNIST OATH

No discussion of the canonical obligation of profession of faith would be complete without a consideration of the oath against Modernism and the profession of faith that is prescribed by it. Although the legislation requiring the oath and the profession of faith antedated the Code by eight years and should, according to the rule of canon 6, 6°, be abolished, since it is not re-enacted, a decision of the Holy Office in 1918 declared that the obligation of taking the oath and making the profession of faith continues in force until the Holy See expressly abrogates it.[1]

This decision was probably prompted by the same reason that led Pope Pius X (1903-1914) to proscribe the evils of Modernism by means of the oath. Modernism is a modern heresy. It saw birth in the last century and made inroads into the personnel of the Church, particularly in France. It is an attempt to rationalize the dogmas of Christianity and to show their inadequacy in the light of modern research. According to Pope Pius X the system is a complex of every heresy. Its proponents, clamoring for emancipation from all ecclesiastical authority, abhor the thought of fixed truth, dogma in the real sense, or knowledge derived from Divine revelation.[2] Numerous Pontifical documents were issued against this heresy, but the most important were those of the above-mentioned Pontiff.

Pius X formulated the errors of Modernism and condemned them, and at the same time prescribed the oath against the heresy in two documents, a constitution, *Pascendi,* and a *motu proprio, Sacrorum antistitum.*[3] The oath is in effect an affirmation of the doctrines of the Church, an admission of her magisterial power, and a condemnation of the false doctrines of Modernism. In the *motu proprio* the following are obliged both to make a profession of faith and take the oath against Modernism:

1. Clerics to be ordained to major orders.

[1] Cf. S.C.S. Off., 22 martii 1918—*AAS,* X, 136.

[2] Cf. the Const., *Pascendi—Fontes,* n. 680; *The New Catholic Dictionary* (New York: The Universal Knowledge Foundation, 1929), p. 641.

[3] *Pascendi* was issued September 8, 1907. It may be found in *Fontes,* n. 680; *Sacrorum antistitum* bears the date of September, 1, 1910. It is to be found in *Fontes,* n. 689.

2. Priests chosen as confessors and preachers, before they receive their faculties to exercise these offices.

3. Pastors, canons, and those appointed to benefices, before they take possession of these benefices.

4. The officials of the Episcopal curia and the ecclesiastical tribunals, not excepting the Vicar General and the judges.

5. Lenten preachers.

6. Officials of the Roman congregations and tribunals, who must take the oath and make the profession before the Cardinal Prefect or secretary of the Congregation or tribunal.

7. Moderators and teachers of religious families and congregations before they assume their office.[4]

According to the same *motu proprio,* moreover, teachers and professors in Catholic universities and seminaries must make the profession of faith and take the oath. That this obligation extends to religious seminaries is confirmed by a decree of the Holy See.[5]

By virtue of this prescription, therefore, those mentioned in canon 1406, § 1, 5°, 7°, 8°, and 9° are required to take the anti-Modernist oath; besides these, all those promoted to benefices, whether the care of souls is attached to these benefices or not; officials in episcopal curias and ecclesiastical tribunals and the judges; Lenten preachers; all the officials of the Roman Tribunals and Congregations and teachers in religious families and congregations must make a profession of faith and take the oath against Modernism. The *motu proprio* rules that the oath is to be taken before the *proper superiors,* which, in most cases, means the Bishop or his delegate for the secular clergy, and the religious superiors for the regulars.[6]

What is in reality effected by the retention of the oath against Modernism is the following:

Subdeacons take the profession of faith before the local Ordinary, as prescribed in canon 1406, § 1, and at the same time take the oath against Modernism. The Holy See has ruled that it is sufficient to

[4] Cf. *Fontes,* n. 689; Coronata, *Institutiones,* II, 352, 353; Wernz-Vidal, *Ius Canonicum,* tom. IV, vol. II, 24.

[5] S.C. Consist., 25 sept. 1910—*AAS,* II, 669.

[6] Cf. Blat, *Commentarium,* III, 431.

have the oath taken only before this order and that it is not necessary to repeat it before diaconate and priesthood.[7]

Priests chosen as confessors and preachers must add to the profession of faith they take before receiving faculties the oath against Modernism. Religious preachers and confessors are bound to this oath as well as seculars and must make it before the local Ordinary, not before the religious superior, even though they receive their faculties from the latter, according to a response of the Holy See that ruled thus.[8] The oath need not be repeated by religious before another Ordinary once it has been taken before a local Ordinary if the same faculties are asked for, e.g., the faculties for preaching and hearing Confessions. Priests of the Oriental disciplines, moreover, are not bound to take the oath before the Ordinaries of a diverse rite from whom they may petition faculties, even though they may not have taken the oath before their own superiors.[9]

Pastors, canons, and those appointed to benefices to which is attached the care of souls may take the oath against Modernism when they make their profession of faith as prescribed by canon 1406, § 1. Those appointed to benefices to which the care of souls is not attached must make a profession of faith and take the oath against Modernism before they obtain possession of these benefices. This latter obligation does not arise from the Code, but does bind by reason of the *motu proprio* under discussion.

The obligation imposed on Lenten preachers to make a profession of faith and take the oath is in addition to the profession and oath they must take before receiving the faculty for preaching. This gives rise to an interesting question: Does the law embrace all Lenten preachers or only those who give a daily sermon during Lent? Vermeersch points out that this legislation has reference to those speakers who daily, throughout the whole of Lent, give discourses on dogmatic, moral, or apologetic subjects. He denies that it refers to those who speak only once a week during Lent, or give an occasional sermon during that season.[10]

This seems to be the correct view on the matter. Certainly the occasional preacher in Lent or the one who comments on one or more of

[7] S.C. Consist., 24 martii 1911—*AAS* III, 181, ad 2.

[8] Cf. S.C. Consist., 17 dec. 1910—*AAS*, III, 25.

[9] Cf. S.C. Consist., 20 iunii 1913—*AAS*, V, 272.

[10] Cf. *Periodica de Re Canonica et Morali utili Praesertim Religiosis et Missionariis* (Bruges, 1905 —),V, 210, in nota.

the Seven Last Words at a "Tre Ore" service is not properly a "Lenten preacher." It seems, moreover, that those assistants in a parish who are called upon once or twice a week to deliver sermons during the Lenten season are not bound by the obligation of making a new profession of faith and taking the oath against Modernism before the local Ordinary. In Europe the custom prior to the war was to have a priest speak daily on the mysteries of religion, the dogmas of the Church, etc., throughout the whole of Lent. These are they, it would seem, to whom the legislation is addressed.

The officials of the episcopal curia and the ecclesiastical tribunals should make a profession of faith and take the oath against Modernism immediately upon appointment to office. These officials are the Vicar General, the judge *(officialis)*, the chancellor, the promoter of justice, the defender of the bond, the synodal judges and examiners, the parochial consultors, the auditors, notaries, and summoners.[11] Since the Vicar General is *ex officio* member of the curia, he need not repeat the profession and oath after he has taken it upon assuming office. The other officials of the diocesan curia, however, are usually chosen from among those who have made profession of faith and taken the oath by reason of some other benefice or dignity. It seems clear from the wording of the *motu proprio* that these are required to make a new profession of faith and take the oath against Modernism upon their appointment to the curia or tribunal. This would be consonant with the prescriptions of canon 1406, § 2, which demands a new profession of faith when one receives a new appointment, even of the same kind.

The Code in canon 1406, § 1, 7°, permits professors of canon law, theology, and philosophy to make a profession of faith only at the beginning of their teaching career, although it counsels that they make it at the beginning of each school year. This toleration of making it only once is in abeyance until the oath against Modernism is no longer required, for *Sacrorum antistitum* demands that teachers and lecturers in seminaries and religious communities take the oath and make the profession yearly, before they begin their lectures.[12]

[11] Cf. canon 363, § 2.

[12] Vermeersch holds that the teachers and lecturers here spoken of are those who teach in theology and philosophy only.—*Periodica,* V, 231. Why he excludes the teachers of canon law is not known, but since the wording of the *motu propio* does not exempt them, there seems no reason to hold his opinion with him.

CHAPTER IX

INFORMAL PROFESSION OF FAITH

Canon 1325.—1. Fideles Christi fidem aperte profiteri tenentur quoties eorum silentium tergiversatio aut ratio agendi secumferrent implicitam fidei negationem, contemptum religionis, iniuriam Dei vel scandalum proximi.

Besides giving a precept to profess the faith in certain positive instances, the Code in the present canon also determines those cases in which an external profession of faith is necessary from the Divine law itself.[1] The obligation that arises from the Divine law is primarily a question of moral theology, not of canon law, but the compilers of the Code evidently considered the precept of external faith so important that they included it under the title which treats of the teaching authority of the Church. It will be the purpose of this chapter, therefore, after treating of the historical aspects of the subject, to study profession of faith from the viewpoint of moral theology.

ARTICLE I. HISTORICAL DEVELOPMENT

Subterfuge to avoid open profession of the faith for the sake of worldly advantage is almost as old as the Church. Some of the early Christians, converts from Judaism, thought it better for the sake of social position or business to make some pretense at Jewish worship. During the time of the persecutions, particularly the latter ones, members of the Church in considerable numbers avoided punishment and loss by seeming compliance with the government's anti-Christian policy, although inwardly they still adhered to the doctrines of the Church.[2] To meet and counteract this fault it was found necessary at a very early date to legislate against it. In the *Canones Apostolorum,* written very probably in the fifth century,[3] very serious penalties against participation in Jewish and pagan worship are to be found, among them excommunication and suspension.[4]

[1] Cf. Coronata, *Institutiones,* II, 247.

[2] Cf. canon 11 of the I Council of Nicaea and a full development of this subject in Schroeder, *Disciplinary Decrees of the General Councils,* pp. 39-41.

[3] Cf. Van Hove, *Prolegomena,* p. 95, n. 109.

[4] Cf. canons 62, 64, 70, and 71.—Hardouin, I, 33-34; Mansi, I, 29-30; Hefele-Clark, I, 475.

That a Christian could offend against faith without necessarily rejecting the faith can be seen from the regulation of the twelfth canon of the I Council of Nicaea, which declared: Those who, called by grace, showed their first zeal by laying aside their military uniforms, but afterwards returned to army service, are to remain for three years among the *audientes* and for ten years among the *substrati.* Now, while military uniforms and army service might have been metaphorical terms to indicate a lapse into heresy or paganism, it is very probable that the canon refers to those Christians who had enlisted in the army of Licinius, the champion of paganism, in the latter's struggle against Constantine. Every Christian who had not left Licinius' army when it had become evident what his purposes were, or who had re-enlisted, was considered a *lapsus,* even though he did not formally apostatize.[5]

The constant surveillance of the Church against even implicit negation of the faith is evident throughout its whole history. Even in comparatively modern times this is evident, as can be seen from the following pronouncements of the Sovereign Pontiffs.

In an instruction, *Sanctissimus,* issued August 13, 1595, Pope Clement VIII declared that the Italo-Greeks, about whose rite the instruction is concerned, were obliged to believe that the Holy Ghost proceeds from the Father and the Son, but allowed them to refrain from including this belief in their Creed unless there was danger of scandal.[6]

Pope Benedict XIV declared in an encyclical dated in 1774 to the priests and people of Serbia that there existed a prohibition against the use of Mohammedan names and customs of the followers of the Prophet, especially against the neglect of Christian days of fast, and the entering of Mohammedan temples, that is, manners by which they might be thought adherents of the sect of Islam. The reason for the prohibition, the Pontiff explained, was that the above-mentioned practices constituted a virtual denial of the faith, an injury to God, and a grave source of scandal.[7] The same Pontiff confirmed the ruling of the constitution, *Inter omnigenas,* in another constitution addressed to the prelates, priests, and missionaries of the Province of Albania. He further prohibited the use of Turkish or Mohammedan names by Christians to avoid persecution and he roundly condemned

[5] Cf. Schroeder, *op. cit.,* p. 41.

[6] Cf. *Fontes,* n. 179.

[7] Const., *Inter omnigenas,* 2 febr. 1774, ad 3—*Fontes,* n. 339. Other decisions on the conduct of Christians in Mohammedan countries are to be found in the decisions of the Sacred Congregation for the Propagation of the Faith. Cf. *Fontes,* nn. 4454, 4562, 4785, 1074, 788, and 994.

those priests who connived at this practice by permitting the faithful with Turkish names to receive the sacraments.[8]

The Sacred Congregations were also very articulate in condemning certain practices of Christians who were attempting to conceal the fact of their faith. On numerous instances they demanded that there be no equivocation in the matter of faith.[9]

One of the most interesting chapters in the whole history of the question is that which arose out of the attempts of missionaries to Christianize China. Christianity and the Jesuits had come to China with St. Francis Xavier and almost immediately began to find favor there. In the reign of K'ang Hsi (1667-1728) many of the Jesuit missionaries, including Adam Schall, Verbiest, Gerbillon, and Bouvet, attained high imperial favor as a result of their scholarship and particularly because Verbiest had turned his scientific abilities into producing weapons for the Emperor's armies. A frank recognition of the services of the Jesuits and words of imperial approval of their attempts to Christianize China were contained in an imperial decree dated March, 1692.

Unfortunately, however, other missionaries, resenting the influence of the Jesuits, complained to Rome that the former were encouraging pagan practices among the Christian converts. The question of the proper term in the Chinese language for God, and the question of whether Chinese Christians could be permitted to observe their ancestral rites and the rites in honor of Confucius proved to be the points at issue. The Jesuit, Matteo Ricci, had taken a position he believed would facilitate the spread of Christianity among the scholars and the officials of the empire. For God he used the word, *T'ien* (heaven) and *Shang Ti* (Supreme Being), expressions frequently used in the Chinese classics, and he took the stand that the ancestral and Confucian sacrifices, having no religious connotation, might properly be performed by Christians.

The Holy See, after first approving of the policy of Ricci, later decided in favor of his opponents. This ended the reign of toleration in the empire and was the beginning of a persecution that lasted intermittently for more than a century.[10]

[8] Cf. Const., *Quod Provinciale,* 1 aug. 1745—*Fontes,* n. 431.

[9] Cf. S.C.S. Off., 19 apr. 1635—*Fontes,* n. 723; 28 aug. 1669—*Fontes,* n. 740; 27 maii 1671—*Fontes,* n. 744; 29 iul. 1699—*Fontes,* n. 762.

[10] Cf. Steiger, *A History of the Far East* (New York: Ginn and Co., 1936), pp. 442-447; Latourette, *A History of Christian Missions in China* (New York: Macmillan & Co., 1929), which treats of the controversy objectively and with considerable acumen.

In view of the foregoing it is interesting to study the following decisions with regard to the conduct of Christians in China during the persecutions:

Christian magistrates were forbidden to honor Confucius by following the practices of the officials, i.e., entering the temples dedicated to this semi-deity, prostrating themselves, and offering candles and incense. Christian Chinese were also forbidden to observe the practice of honoring their ancestors at rites performed twice a year in the temples dedicated to Confucius.[11]

To show their contempt for Christianity the pagans of one part of China carved crosses on the public streets so that it was nearly impossible not to tread upon them. The Christians asked whether they could be allowed to walk on these crosses on some occasions, because it was virtually impossible not to do so, though by so doing they might deceive some of their neighbors as to their true religious status. The response was that Christians should never walk on the crosses unless it was impossible not to do so, and then only if they showed by their reverence that they were followers of the cross. It was decided, moreover, that the Christian Chinese could never use the circumstance of their walking on the crosses to deceive their neighbors as to their religious status.[12]

Other decisions prohibited Catholic mandarins from honoring Confucius despite the fact they held a concealed crucifix in their hand and made all reverences to it;[13] forbade Christians to sign an ambiguous document in which they promised not to join any false religion,[14] and restrained candidates for the doctorate from bribing judges so they might not have to go through the ceremonial of honoring Confucius.[15]

The response of the Sacred Congregation for the Propagation of the Faith that will be finally considered is that which denied missionaries permission to sign a notice issued by some lenient mandarins in order that exile rather than death might be the missionaries' lot, since this

[11] Cf. S.C.S. Off., 13 nov. 1669—*Fontes*, nn. 741 and 730. Regarding ancestor honor see also a response of the same Congregation dated August 20, 1776 —*Fontes*, n. 836.

[12] Cf. C.S.C. Off., instr. *(ad Vic. Ap. Hun-nan)*, 1863—*Collectanea S. Congregationis de Propaganda Fide*, I, n. 1055.

[13] Cf. S.C. de Prop. Fide, *(Sinarum)*, 12 sept., 1645, §§ 7, 8—*Fontes*, n. 4459.

[14] Cf. S.C. de Prop Fide, *(C.P. pro Sin.)*, 7 febr. 1791 et 4 ian. 1798—*Collectanea*, I, nn. 604 et 643.

[15] *Loc. cit.*

notice declared that the missionaries were not priests or preachers of an alien faith.[16]

In the light of these decisions and remembering the dispute between the Jesuits and other missionaries in the seventeenth century regarding the Chinese rites, it is extremely interesting to review the very recent decisions of the Holy See on the matter.

In a private response to the Vicars Apostolic of Kirin, Manchukuo, May 28, 1935, the Sacred Congregation of the Propagation of Faith declared as follows:

It is lawful to expose the image of Confucius in the schools of the missions if the lawful authorities of the country so order. It is permitted the students to make a more or less profound inclination before the image thus exposed if the authorities demand this. The reason for these decisions lies in the fact that the cult paid to Confucius is merely civil in character. The Sacred Congregation also permitted, in cases of grave necessity, that Christians in the service of the authorities might fulfill the minor duties of sacrifice to Confucius, provided that the co-operation was merely material. Financial co-operation in the repair or construction of pagodas in honor of Confucius was also tolerated, as was the salute to the dead formerly forbidden, since this had lost its religious character.[17]

In a decree dated May 26, 1936, the same Sacred Congregation also declared in favor of certain Japanese rites that had once been considered religious in character, e.g., the visiting of the national temples or Jinja, and the participation in funerals, marriages, and other private rites. The reason for this decision, it was declared, was that such acts were patriotic or social and in no way connected with religious observance.[18] A third decree was issued in February, 1940, when the Holy See repeated in substance the decrees mentioned above and revoked the oath which had been imposed on missionaries for more than a century by which they promised to refrain from controversy on the Chinese rites question.[19]

Article II. Moral Obligation

Profession of faith is its external manifestation before men by

[16] Cf. *Collectanea,* n. 776.

[17] Bouscaren, *Canon Law Digest,* II, 161-164.

[18] Bouscaren, *Digest,* II, 164-166; *AAS,* XXVIII, 406.

[19] Cf. *AAS,* XXXII, 24, sqq.

words or facts. It is commanded by both Divine and ecclesiastical law.[20] St. Paul says:

> For if thou confess with thy mouth that Jesus is the Lord, and believe it in thy heart that God has raised him from the dead, thou shalt be saved. For with the heart a man believes unto justice, and with the mouth profession of faith is made unto salvation.[21]

Our Divine Lord Himself has said:

> Therefore everyone who acknowledges me before men, I also will acknowledge him before my Father in heaven. But whoever disowns me before men, I in turn will disown him before my Father in heaven.[22]

The principal reason why God has commanded that an exterior profession of faith be made are these: Christ founded a Church which is visible in itself and is endowed with a visible worship. Hence the members of that Church should manifest the fact of their membership in an external, visible manner, i. e., by profession of faith. That Christian, moreover, would commit a grave irreverence towards God and would be guilty of the worst ingratitude who because of vain human fear would hide the fact that he is a faithful servant and worshipper of the one, true God. An external profession of faith, finally, helps to strengthen interior faith and is often the means of converting those who are tepid in faith or even infidels.[23]

Profession of faith is distinguished into material and formal profession. The former is made when one leads a truly Christian life, for by such habitual conduct one clearly manifests his faith. Formal profession is an explicitly intended declaration of faith. This profession must be made, according to the natural law, when it is the only means whereby the honor due to God or the faith of one's neighbor may be preserved from harm, or acts contrary to charity

[20] Cf. Prümmer, *Manuale Theologiae Moralis* (3 vols., 8. ed., Friburgi Brisgoviae: Herder, 1935), I, 354; Merkelbach, *Summa Theologiae Moralis* (3 vols., 2. ed., Paris: Desclee de Brouwer, 1935), I, 553; Noldin, *Summa Theologiae Moralis Iuxta Codicem Iuris Canonici* (3 vols., 20. ed., Oeniponte: Pustet, 1930), II, 19; Konings, *Theologia Moralis Sancti Alphonsi in Compendium Redacta* (2 vols., 7. ed., Einsidlae, 1888), I, 110; Gury, *Compendium Theologiae Moralis* (4. ed., Ratisbonae, 1868), p. 87.

[21] Rom., X, 9, 10, 11.

[22] Matt. X, 32, 33.

[23] Cf. Prümmer, *Manuale*, I, 354.

towards God or one's neighbor may be prevented.[24] The precept of profession of faith is, moreover, affirmative and negative. In so far as it is negative it prohibits one from exteriorly denying his faith either expressly or tacitly, by word, sign, or deed, for any cause, even to escape death. The negative precept also prohibits one from adhering to a false religion or simulating adherence to such a religion. One who would ignore this negative precept would at least implicitly affirm that God either revealed false doctrines or that He had not revealed the dogmas of the Christian religion.[25] The negative precept of profession of faith can be violated directly and explicitly, when one knowingly denies the Christian faith or professes a false one, or indirectly and implicitly, when one without the intention of denying the faith does something that would be considered as a negation of faith by others, e.g., when he formally participates in heretical rites.

One can sin against faith, therefore, in the following ways:

1. If one, either seriously or fictitiously, would reject even one article of the faith; would deny that he is a Christian or a Catholic; would affirm that he belongs to another sect, or would deny that he is a "Papist" or an adherent of the Church described by other such names in those regions where the words are meant to signify only a member of the Catholic Church.

2. If one would try to conceal the fact of his religious adherence by using rites or ceremonies of a false sect, e.g., if he would participate in the Lord's Supper in some Protestant sect, offer incense to or genuflect before heathen idols, or use circumcision as a religious rite.

3. If one would buy testimonials that he had professed a false religion.

4. If one would place an action which of itself or from the circumstances in which it was placed would signify the profession of a false religion, e.g., if he would participate in a toast to the death of all Catholics or to the health of the enemies of the Church; would pray with non-Catholics; would give his name to heretical sects; or would join the Free Masons or other anti-Catholic societies.

5. Generally, if one would use the special vesture that signifies that the wearer is a professed member of some false sect.

[24] Vermeersch, *Theologia Moralis* (3. ed., 3 vols., Romae: Universitas Gregorianae, 1937), II, 14.

[25] Cf. Merkelbach, *Summa Theologiae Moralis,* I, 553; Prümmer, op. cit., 354-355; Noldin, *Summa,* II, 19.

6. Generally, if one would remain silent or use ambiguous words when questioned concerning his religion by the public authorities, for this mode of acting, in the common estimation of men, is considered to be a denial of the faith or a sign that the one being questioned is ashamed of the fact that he is a follower of Christ.

With regard to the last two classifications, it is possible that because of peculiar circumstances neither the wearing of special vesture or taciturnity when questioned about one's religion would constitute a denial of faith.[26]

In so far as the precept of confessing one's faith is affirmative, an external profession of faith is always demanded, even if death would be the result, in the following cases:

1. When the omission of this confession would result in an infringement on the honor due to God. Hence, not only must the one interrogated about his faith by public authority confess it when by remaining silent he would be considered a heretic, but he must prevent, if possible, the misuse of sacred things by heretics and infidels. Likewise, he who hears the Church being attacked by her enemies must answer the objections and refute the misstatements if he is well enough informed to do this; or, if not, he must at least make a profession of his faith if he sees that this course of action would be effective.[27]

2. When the spiritual good of one's neighbor demands that a profession of faith be made, or when otherwise grave scandal, contempt of religion, or perversion would result. This would be the case, for example, when if one were to remain silent about his religion it would lead another to believe that he had abandoned his faith, or thought it of little worth, and hence would result in the weakening of the latter's faith or of his desire for conversion.[28]

The negative precept of confession of faith obliges always and admits of no exceptions (*obligat semper et pro semper*).[29] Since, however, the affirmative precept does not oblige at all times, the following generally do not sin against faith by words, signs, or deeds:

1. Those who for a serious reason conceal their faith or dissimulate

[26] Cf. Merkelbach, *Summa*, I, 554.

[27] Cf. Merkelbach, *loc. cit.;* Prümmer, *op. cit.*, 355; Noldin, *op. cit.*, II, 19, 20.

[28] Cf. Prümmer, *loc. cit.*

[29] Cf. Noldin, *op. cit.*, 22.

about the faith. (It must be remembered that only in extraordinary circumstances can this be permitted.)[80]

2. Those who are asked about their faith by private individuals and who refuse to answer or who use equivocal words in responding.

3. Those who deny or conceal the fact that they are priests, religious, etc.

4. Those who, lest they be thought Catholics, eat meat on Friday, do not assist at Mass, etc., unless these acts are directly interpreted as contempt of religion, disobedience to the Church, or the profession of a false religion.

5. Those who for a very grave cause use the vesture or signs of a nation where such vesture and signs are only probably distinctive of the adherents of a false sect, e.g., in Mohammedan countries.

6. Those who flee in time of persecution, with the exception of pastors of souls whose flight would expose his people to spiritual danger.

7. Those who by payment of money dissuade the enemies of the Church from persecuting them because of their faith or from making inquiries into their faith.

8. Those who fail to comply with the orders of the government which commands that all who are Catholics make themselves known.

It is to be noted that, generally speaking, the persons listed above do not sin against the positive precept of profession of faith. It is very possible that owing to special circumstances any of the abovementioned actions would be tantamount to a negation of faith or an indication that the person who resorted to them was ashamed of his faith. Such actions might well involve an infringement on the honor due to God or an occasion of spiritual harm to one's neighbor. In either case, they would, of course, be prohibited by the natural law.[81]

FINIS

[80] Prümmer (*op. cit.,* 355, nota 45) says: "Nonnulli auctores . . . permittunt indirectam negationem fidei, dummodo adsint sufficientes rationes. Qui quidem modus loquendi, quamvis recte intelligi queat, melius vitatur, cum male sonet et ansam praebeat errandi."

[81] Cf. Noldin, Prümmer, et Merkelbach, *loc. cit.*

PARTICULAR CONCLUSIONS

1. Profession of faith is an essential condition for the exercise of jurisdiction of a Vicar Capitular or diocesan administrator in the government of a vacant diocese.

2. The dignitaries mentioned in canon 1406, § 1, 5°, are not those who are honored by the Holy See by being created Papal Chamberlains, Domestic Prelates, or Protonotaries Apostolic, but those who are members of a Cathedral chapter who have special pre-eminence.

3. Not only pastors, but also vicars, administrators, adjutants, chaplains, if they are appointed with all the rights and duties of pastors, and rectors of oratories must make a profession of faith upon appointment.

4. Unless they have a special indult, members of clerical institutes who receive faculties from their religious superiors for ministering to the members of their own orders or congregations through the hearing of Confessions or through preaching must make a profession of faith before the local Ordinary.

5. The professors contemplated by canon 1406, § 1, 8°, are Catholic teachers. Non-Catholics who hold teaching positions in Pontifical universities are not expected to make a profession of faith, nor expected to be employed without a Papal indult.

6. The loss of revenue that is prescribed as a penalty by canon 2403 for those who neglect to make a profession of faith begins only when they become legally contumacious, i. e., when the time allotted by a competent superior to make the profession of faith has expired.

BIBLIOGRAPHY

Sources

Acta Apostolicae Sedis, Commentarium Officiale, Romae, 1909 —.

Acta et Decreta Concilii Plenarii Baltimorensis III, Baltimorae, 1894.

Acta et Decreta Sacrorum Conciliorum Recentiorum, Collectio Lacensis, Friburgi Brisgoviae, 1870-1890.

Acta Sanctae Sedis, 41 vols., Romae, 1865-1908.

Bullarum Diplomatum et Privilegiorum Sanctorum Romanorum Pontificum Taurinensis Editio, 25 vols., Augustae Taurinorum, 1857-1872.

Bullarii Romani Continuatio Summorum Pontificum, 19 vols., Prati, 1756-1883.

Bullarium SSmi. Domini nostri Benedicti XIV, 4 vols., 4 ed., Venice, 1778.

Canones et Decreta Concilii Tridentini ex Editione Romana A. MDCCCXXXIV Repetiti, editio Neapolitana, Neapoli, 1859.

Codex Iuris Canonici Pii X Pontificis Maximi iussu digestus Benedicti XV auctoritate promulgatus, Romae: Typis Polyglottis Vaticanis, 1917.

Codex Theodosianus, 3 vols., ed. P. Kreuger, Th. Mommsen, P. M. Meyer, Berlin, 1905.

Codicis Iuris Canonici Fontes cura Emi. Petri Card. Gasparri Editi, 9 vols., Romae (Postea Civitate Vaticana): Typis Polyglottis Vaticanis, 1923-1939. (Vols. VII, VIII, et IX ed. cura et studio Emi. Iustiniani Card. Serédi.)

Collectanea S. Congregationis de Propaganda Fide, 2 vols., *Romae,* 1907.

Concilii Plenarii Baltimorensis II Acta et Decreta, Baltimorae, 1894.

Corpus Iuris Canonici, 2 vols., ed. Lipsiensis 2., post Aemilii Ludovici Richteri curas instruxit—Aemilius Friedberg, 2 vols., 1879-1881, ed. anastatice repetita, Lipsiae: Tauchnitz, 1928.

Corpus Iuris Civilis (Kreuger-Mommsen-Schoell-Kroll), 3 vols., Berolini: apud Weidmannos, 1928-1929. Vol. I, *Institutiones,* editio stereotypa 15., 1929, recognoirt Paulus Krueger; ——————*Digesta,* recognovit Theodorus Mommsen, retractavit Paulus Krueger; Vol. II, *Codex Instinianus,* ed. stereotypa 10., 1929, recognovit et retractavit Paulus Krueger; Vol. III, *Novellae,* editio stereotypa 5., 1928, recognovit Rudolfus Schoell; opus Schoellii morte interceptum absolvit Gulielmus Kroll.

Decretales D. Gregorii Papae IX, una cum Glossa Restitutae, Romae, 1582.

Denzinger, Henr., et Bannwart, Clem., *Enchiridion Symbolorum, Definitionum et Declarationum de Rebus Fidei et Morum,* 18.-20., ed., Friburgi Brisgoviae: Herder, 1928.

Friedberg, Aemilius, *Quinque Compilationes Antiquae,* Lipsiae, 1882.

Hartzheim, *Concilia Germaniae,* 11 vols., Coloniae Augustae Agrippinensium, 1759-1790.

Hardouin, Jean, *Acta Conciliorum et Epistolae Decretales ac Constitutiones Summorum Pontificum,* 12 vols., Parisiis, 1715.

Jaffé, Philippus, *Regesta Pontificum Romanorum ab condita Ecclesia ad annum post Christum natum MCXCVIII,* 2 vols. in 1, Lipsiae, 1885-1888.

Mansi, Joannes, *Sacrorum Conciliorum Nova et Amplissima Collectio,* 53 vols. in 59, Parisiis, 1901-1927.

Pallottini, Salvator, *Collectio Omnium Conclusionum et Resolutionum Congregationis Concilii ab anno 1564-1860,* 18 vols., Romae, 1868-1895.

Pontificale Romanum, Ratisbonae, 1891.

Potthast, Aug., *Regesta Romanorum Pontificum inde ab anno post Christum natum MCXCVIII ad MCCCIV,* 2 vols., Berolini, 1874-1875.

Rituale Romanum, editio Vaticana, Taurini-Romae: Marietti, 1926.

Thesaurus Resolutionum Sacrae Congregationis Concilii, 167 vols., Romae, 1718-1908.

Reference Works

Aertnys, Jas., Damen, C.A., *Theologia Moralis,* 2 vols., 11. ed., Taurinorum Augustae: Marietti, 1928.

Aquinas, St. Thomas, *Divi Thomae Aquinatis Opera,* 2. ed. Veneta, 28 vols., Venetiis, 1775-1788.

Augustinus, Antonius, *Antiquae Decretalium Collectiones Commentariis et Emendationibus Illustratae,* Parisiis, 1621.

(Bachofen), Charles Augustine, *A Commentary on the New Code of Canon Law,* 8 vols., St. Louis: Herder & Co., 1925-1938. Vol. I, 6. ed., 1931; vol. II, 6. ed., 1936; vol. III, 5. ed., 1938; vol. IV, 3. ed., 1925; vol. V, 5. ed., 1935; vol. VI, 3. ed., 1931; vol. VII, 3, ed., 1930; vol. VIII, 3. ed., 1931.

Ayrinhac, H. A., *Administrative Legislation in the New Code of Canon Law,* New York: Longmans Green and Co., 1930.

Barbosa, Augustinus, *Summa Apostolicarum Decisionum,* Lugduni, 1695.

Benedictus XIV, *De Synodo Dioecesana,* 2 vols., Romae, 1806.

——— *Institutiones Ecclesiasticae,* Romae, 1747.

Beste, Udalricus, *Introductio in Codicem,* Collegeville, Minn.: St. John's Abbey Press, 1938.

Blat, Albertus, *Commentarium Texus Codicis Iuris Canonici,* 5 vols. in 7, Romae: Collegio "Angelico," 1921-1938. Vol. 1, 1921; vol. II, pars I, ed. altera, 1921; vol. II, partes II et III, 3. ed., 1938; vol. III, pars I, 2. ed., 1924; vol. III, partes II et III, 2. ed., 1934; vol. IV, 1927; vol. V, 1924.

Bouscaren, T. Lincoln, *Canon Law Digest,* 2 vols., and 2 supplements—1938 and 1941, Milwaukee: Bruce, 1934-1941.

Catholic Encyclopedia, The, 15 vols., New York, 1907-1912.

Chelodi, Ioannes, *Ius Poenale,* 4. ed., Tridenti: Libreria Moderna Editrice, A. Ardesi, 1935.

Cicognani, Amleto G., *Canon Law,* 2. revised edition, authorized English version, translated by J. M. O'Hara and F. Brennan, Philadelphia: Dolphin Press, 1935.

Cocchi, Guidus, *Commentarium in Codicem Iuris Canonici ad Usum Scholarum,* 5 vols. in 8, Taurinorum Augustae: Marietti, 1931-1938.

Coronata, Matthaeus Conte a, *Institutiones Iuris Canonici,* 5 vols., Taurini: Marietti, 1928-1939.

Creusen, Joseph—Garesche, Edward—Ellis, Adam, *Religious Men and Women in the Code,* Milwaukee: Bruce, 1940.

DeMeester, Alphonsus, *Juris Canonici et Juris Canonico-Civilis Compendium,* nova ed., 3 vols. in 4, Brugis, 1921-1928.

De Rozière, Eugene, *Liber Diurnus ou Recueil Général des Formules Usitees par la Chancellerie Pontificale du V au XI Siècle*, Paris, 1869.

Eichmann, E., *Das Strafrecht des Codex Iuris Canonici*, Paderborn, 1920.

Fanfani, L. I., *De Iure Religiosorum*, Taurini-Romae: Marietti, 1925.

Feldhaus, Aloysius, *Oratories*, Catholic University of America Canon Law Studies, No. 42, Washington, D.C.; The Catholic University of America, 1927.

Fournier, Paul—Le Bras, Gabriel, *Histoire des Collections Canoniques en Occident*, 2 vols., Paris: Recuiel Sirey, 1931.

Garnier, P., *Liber Diurnus Romanorum Pontificum ex Antiquissimo Codice Manuscripto Nunc Primum in Lucem Editus*, parisiis, 1680—In *MPL*, CV.

Grandclaude, E., *Ius Canonicum Juxta Ordinem Decretalium Recentioribus Sedis Apostolicae Decretis et Rectae Rationi in Omnibus Consonium*, 3 vols., Parisiis, 1882-1883.

Guilday, P., *A History of the Councils of Baltimore*, New York: The Macmillan Co., 1932.

Gury, J., *Compendium Theologiae Moralis*, 4. ed., Ratisbonae, 1868.

Hinschius, Paul, *Das Kirchenrecht der Katholichen und Protestanten in Deutschland*, 6 vols., Berlin, 1869-1897.

————, *Decretales Pseudo-Isidoriana*, Lipsiae, 1863.

Hefele-Clark, *History of the Christian Councils*, 5 vols., Edinburgh, 1883-1896.

Ivo of Chartres, *Decretum*—in *MPL*, CLXI; *Panormia*—*MPL*, CLXI.

Konings, J., *Theologia Moralis Sancti Alphonsi in Compendium Redacta*, 2 vols., 7. ed., Einsidlae, 1888.

Latourette, K. S., *A History of Christian Missions in China*, New York: The Macmillan Co., 1929.

Lortz-Kaiser, *History of the Church*, Milwaukee: Bruce, 1938.

Lupus, Christianus, *Synodorum Generalium ac Provinvialium Decreta et Canones*, 9 vols., Venetii, 1724-1727.

Merkelbach, B. H., *Summa Theologiae Moralis*, 3 vols., 2. ed., Paris: Desclée de Brouwer, 1935.

Messmer, S. G., *Praxis Synodalis*, 2. ed., New York, 1886.

Michiels, Gommarus, *Normae Generales Iuris Canonici*, 2 vols., Lublin: Universitas Catholica, 1929.

Migne, Jacques Paul, *Patrologiae Cursus Completus, Series Graeca*, 161 vols., Parisiis, 1857-1866.

————, *Patrologiae Cursus Completus, Series Latina*, 221 vols., Parisiis, 1844-1855.

————, *Theologiae Cursus Completus*, 28 vols., Parisiis, 1863-1866.

McVann, James, *The Canon Law of Sermon Preaching*, New York: The Paulist Press, 1940.

New Catholic Dictionary, The, New York: The Universal Knowledge Foundation, 1929.

Noldin, H.-Schmitt, A., *Summa Theologiae Moralis Iuxta Codicem Iuris Canonici*, 3 vols., 21. ed., Oeniponte, 1932.

Ojetti, B., *Synopsis Rerum Moralium et Iuris Pontificii*, Romae, 1899.

Pastor, Ludwig Freiherr von, *The History of the Popes From the Close of the Middle Ages,* 32 vols., translation, vols. I-VI, ed. by Frederick I. Antrobus; vols. VII-XXIV, ed. by Ralph F. Kerr; vols. XXV-XXXII, ed., by Dom Ernest Graf, St. Louis: Herder, 1906-1940.

Prümmer, D. M., *Manuale Iuris Canonici,* 3. ed., Friburgi Brisgoviae: Herder, 1922.

———, *Manuale Theologiae Moralis,* 8. ed., 3 vols., Friburgi Brisgoviae: Herder, 1935.

Reiffenstuel, Anacletus, *Ius Canonicum Universum,* 5 vols. in 7, Parisiis, 1864-1870.

Schmalzgrueber, Franciscus, *Ius Ecclesiasticum Universum,* 5 vols. in 12, Romae, 1843-1845.

Schroeder, H. J., *Disciplinary Decrees of the General Councils,* St. Louis: Herder, 1937.

Steiger, G. Nye, *A History of the Far East,* New York: Ginn & Co., 1936.

Van Hove, A., *Commentarium Lovaniense in Codicem Iuris Canonici,* vol. I, tom. I, *Prolegomena ad Codicem Iuris Canonici,* Mechliniae: H. Dessain, 1928.

———, *De Legibus Ecclesiasticis,* 1930.

———, *De Rescriptis,* 1936.

Vermeersch, A.-Creusen, J., *Epitome Iuris Canonici,* 3 vols., tom. I, 6. ed., 1937; toms. II-III, 5. ed., 1936, Mechliniae-Romae: H. Dessain.

Vermeersch, A., *Theologia Moralis,* 3. ed., 3 vols., Romae: Universitas Gregorianae, 1937.

Wernz, F. X., *Ius Decretalium,* 6 vols., Romae et Prati, 1898-1906.

Wernz-Vidal, *Ius Decretalium,* 7 vols. in 8, Romae: Apud Aedes Universitatis Gregorianae, 1923-1938.

Woywod, S., *A Practical Commentary on the Code of Canon Law,* 5. ed., 2 vols., New York: Jos. F. Wagner, 1939.

Principal Articles

D' Angelo, Sosius, "De Professione Fidei," *Apollinaris,* Romae, I (1928), 415-417.

Kuttner, Stephan, "The Father of the Science of Canon Law," *The Jurist,* Catholic University of America, Washington, D. C., I (1941), 2-19.

Pietz, W., "Liber Diurnus," *Sitzungsberichte der Kais. Akademie der Wissenschaften in Wien, phil.-hist. Cl.,* CLXXXV, n. 4, I, 144.

"Profession of Faith Before Taking Possession of a Parish," *Australasian Catholic Record,* X (1933), p. 147.

Santifaller, W., "Zur Liber Diurnus-Forschung," *Historische Zeitschrift,* CLXI, pp. 535, sqq.

Sickel, Th. R., "Prolegomena zum Liber Diurnus I und II," *Sitzungsberichte der kais. Akademie der Wissenschaften in Wien, phil.-hist. Cl.,* CXVII, VII, 1-76; XIII, 1-94.

Vidal, P., "Il Nuovo Codice di Diritto Canonico," *Civiltá Cattolica,* anno 68 (1917), p. 557.

Woywod, S., "The Profession of Faith," *Homiletic and Pastoral Review,* XXVIII (1928), 1179-1187.

Periodicals

Analecta Iuris Pontificii, Romae, 1855-1868; Parisiis, 1869-1891.
Apollinaris, Romae, 1928—.
Australasian Catholic Record, The, Manly, N.S.W., 1923—.
Civiltá Cattolica, Roma, 1850—.
Historische Zeitschrift, München und Berlin, 1836—.
Homiletic and Pastoral Review, The, New York, 1900—.
Jurist, The, Washington, D. C., 1941—.
Periodica de Re Canonica et Morali utili Praesertim Religiosis et Missionariis, Bruges, 1905—.
Sitzungsberichte der kais. Akademie der Wissenschaften in Wien, phil.-hist. Classe, Vienna, 1847—.

Abbreviations

AAS—*Acta Apostolicae Sedis.*
AIP—*Analecta Iuris Pontificii.*
ASS—*Acta Sanctae Sedis.*
C.—*Codex* (Iustinianus).
c.—Canon.
cc.—Canones.
Coll. Lac.—*Acta et Decreta Conciliorum Recentiorum, Collectio Lacensis.*
D.—*Digesta* (Iustiniana).
Fontes—*Codicis Iuris Canonici Fontes cura . . . Gasparri Editi.*
Hardouin—*Acta Conciliorum,* etc.
Mansi—*Sacrorum Conciliorum Nova et Amplissima Collectio.*
MPG—Migne, *Patrologia Graeca.*
MPL—Migne, *Patrologia Latina.*
N.—*Novellae* (Iustinianae).
PCI—Pontificia Commissio Interpretationis.
Periodica—*Periodica de Re Canonica et Morali.*
S.C.C.—Sacra Congregatio Concilii.
S. C. Consist.—Sacra Congregatio Consistorialis.
S. C. de Prop. Fide—Sacra Congregatio de Propaganda Fide.
S.C.S. Off.—Sacra Congregatio Sancti Officii.

BIOGRAPHICAL NOTE

WALTER JOSEPH CANAVAN was born on Dec. 5, 1909, in Denver, Colorado. After receiving his primary education in St. Joseph's school there, he entered St. Joseph's Preparatory college, Kirkwood, Missouri, and was graduated from that institution in 1927. His philosophical and theological courses were pursued at St. Thomas' seminary in Denver, Colorado, and he was ordained to the priesthood by the Most Rev. Urban J. Vehr May 26, 1934. He was sent to the Catholic University of America in 1939 and received the Baccalaureate in Canon Law from that institution in June, 1940, and the Licentiate in Canon Law from the same institution in June, 1941.

ALPHABETICAL INDEX

CANON LAW STUDIES

1. Freriks, Rev. Celestine A., C.PP.S., J.C.D., Religious Congregations in Their External Relations, 121 pp., 1916.
2. Galliher, Rev. Daniel M., O.P., J.C.D., Canonical Elections, 117 pp., 1917.
3. Borkowski, Rev. Aurelius L., O.F.M., J.C.D., De Confraternitatibus Ecclesiasticis, 136 pp., 1918.
4. Castillo, Rev. Cayo, J.C.D., Disertacion Historico-Canonica sobre la Potestad del Cabildo en Sede Vacante o Impedida del Vicario Capitular, 99 pp., 1919 (1918).
5. Kubelbeck, Rev. William J., S.T.B., J.C.D., The Sacred Penitentiaria and its Relations to Faculties of Ordinaries and Priests, 129 pp., 1918.
6. Petrovits, Rev. Joseph, J.C., S.T.D., J.C.D., The New Church Law On Matrimony, X-461 pp., 1919.
7. Hickey, Rev. John J., S.T.B., J.C.D., Irregularities and Simple Impediments in the New Code of Canon Law, 100 pp., 1920.
8. Klekotka, Rev. Peter J., S.T.B., J.C.D., Diocesan Consultors, 179 pp., 1920.
9. Wanenmacher, Rev. Francis, J.C.D., The Evidence in Ecclesiastical Procedure Affecting the Marriage Bond, 1920 (Printed 1935).
10. Golden, Rev. Henry Francis, J.C.D., Parochial Benefices in the New Code, IV-119 pp., 1921 (Printed 1925).
11. Koudelka, Rev. Charles J., J.C.D., Pastors, Their Rights and Duties According to the New Code of Canon Law, 211 pp., 1921.
12. Melo, Rev. Antonius, O.F.M., J.C.D., De Exemptione Regularium, X-188 pp., 1921.
13. Schaaf, Rev. Valentine Theodore, O.F.M., S.T.B., J.C.D., The Cloister, X-180 pp., 1921.
14. Burke, Rev. Thomas Joseph, S.T.D., J.C.D., Competence in Ecclesiastical Tribunals, IV-117 pp., 1922.
15. Leech, Rev. George Leo, J.C.D., A Comparative Study of the Constitution, "Apostolicae Sedis" and the "Codex Juris Canonici," 179 pp., 1922.
16. Motry, Rev. Hubert Louis, S.T.D., J.C.D., Diocesan Faculties According ing to the Code of Canon Law, II-167 pp., 1922.
17. Murphy, Rev. George Lawrence, J.C.D., Delinquencies and Penalties in the Administration and Reception of the Sacraments, IV-121 pp., 1923.
18. O'Reilly, Rev. John Anthony, S.T.D., J.C.D., Ecclesiastical Sepulture in the New Code of Canon Law, II-129 pp., 1923.
19. Michalicka, Rev. Wenceslas Cyril, O.S.B., J.C.D., Judicial Procedure in Dismissal of Clerical Exempt Religious, 107 pp., 1923.
20. Dargin, Rev. Edward Vincent, S.T.B., J.C.D., Reserved Cases According to the Code of Canon Law, IV-103, pp. 1924.
21. Godfrey, Rev. John A., S.T.B., J.C.D., The Right of Patronage According to the Code of Canon Law, 153 pp., 1924.
22. Hagedorn, Rev. Francis Edward, J.C.D., General Legislation on Indulgences, II-154 pp., 1924.

23. King, Rev. James Ignatius, J.C.D., The Administration of the Sacraments to Dying Non-Catholics, V-141 pp., 1924.

24. Winslow, Rev. Francis Joseph, O.F.M., J.C.D., Vicars and Prefects Apostolic, IV-149 pp., 1924.

25. Correa, Rev. Jose Servelion, S.T.L., J.C.D., La Potestad Legislativa de la Iglesia Catolica, IV-127 pp., 1925.

26. Dugan, Rev. Henry Francis, A.M., J.C.D., The Judiciary Department of the Diocesan Curia, 87 pp., 1925.

27. Keller, Rev. Charles Frederick, S.T.B., J.C.D., Mass Stipends, 167 pp., 1925.

28. Paschang, Rev. John Linus, J.C.D., The Sacramentals According to the Code of Canon Law, 129 pp., 1925.

29. Piontek, Rev. Cyrillus, O.F.M., S.T.B., J.C.D., De Indulto Exclaustrationis necnon Saecularizationis, XIII-289 pp., 1925.

30. Kearney, Rev. Richard Joseph, S.T.B., J.C.D., Sponsors at Baptism According to the Code of Canon Law, IV-127 pp., 1925.

31. Bartlett, Rev. Chester Joseph, A.M., LL.B., J.C.D., The Tenure of Parochial Property in the United States of America, V-108 pp., 1926.

32. Kilker, Rev. Adrian Jerome, J.C.D., Extreme Unction, V-425 pp., 1926.

33. McCormick, Rev. Robert Emmett, J.C.D., Confessors of Religious, VIII-266 pp., 1926.

34. Miller, Rev. Newton Thomas, J.C.D., Founded Masses According to the Code of Canon Law, VII-93 pp., 1926.

35. Roelker, Rev. Edward G., S.T.D., J.C.D., Principles of Privilege According to the Code of Canon Law, XI-166 pp., 1926.

36. Bakalarczyk, Rev. Richardus, M.I.C., J.U.D., De Novitiatu, VIII-208 pp., 1927.

37. Pizzuti, Rev. Lawrence, O.F.M., J.U.L., De Parochis Religiosis, 1927 (Not printed).

38. Bliley, Rev. Nicholas Martin, O.S.B., J.C.D., Altars According to the Code of Canon Law, XIX-132 pp., 1927.

39. Brown, Mr. Brendan Francis, A.B., LL.M., J.U.D., The Canonical Juristic Personality with Special Reference to Its Status in the United States of America, V-212 pp., 1927.

40. Cavanaugh, Rev. William Thomas, C.P., J.U.D., The Reservation of the Blessed Sacrament, VIII-101 pp., 1927.

41. Doheny, Rev. William J., C.S.C., A.B., J.U.D., Church Property: Modes of Acquisition, X-118 pp., 1927.

42. Feldhaus, Rev. Aloysius H., C.PP.S., J.C.D., Oratories, IX-141 pp., 1927.

43. Kelly, Rev. James Patrick, A.B., J.C.D., The Jurisdiction of the Simple Confessor, X-208 pp., 1927.

44. Neuberger, Rev. Nicholas J., J.C.D., Canon 6 or the Relation of the Codex Juris Canonici to the Preceding Legislation, V-95 pp., 1927.

45. O'Keefe, Rev. Gerald Michael, J.C.D., Matrimonial Dispensations, Powers of Bishops, Priests and Confessors, VIII-232 pp., 1927.

46. Quigley, Rev. Joseph, A.B., A.M., J.C.D., Condemned Societies, 139 pp., 1927.

47. Zaplotnik, Rev. Johannes Leo, J.C.D., De Vicariis Foraneis, X-142 pp., 1927.

48 Duskie, Rev. John Aloysius, A.B., J.C.D., The Canonical Status of the Orientals in the United States, VII, 196 pp., 1928.

49. Hyland, Rev. Francis Edward, J.C.D., Excommunication, Its Nature, Historical Development and Effects, VIII-181 pp., 1928.

50. Reinmann, Rev. Gerald Joseph, O.M.C., J.C.D., The Third Order Secular of Saint Francis, 201 pp., 1928.

51. Schenk, Rev. Francis J., J.C.D., The Matrimonial Impediments of Mixed Religion and Disparity of Cult, XVI-318 pp., 1929.

52. Coady, Rev. John Joseph, S.T.D., J.U.D., A.M., The Appointment of Pastors, VIII-150 pp., 1929.

53. Kay, Thomas Henry, J.C.D., Competence in Matrimonial Procedure, VIII-164 pp., 1929.

54. Turner, Rev. Sidney Joseph, C.P., J.U.D., The Vow of Poverty, XLIX-217 pp., 1929.

55. Kearney, Rev. Raymond A., A.B., S.T.D., J.C.D., The Principles of Delegation, VII-149 pp., 1929.

56. Conran, Rev. Edward James, A.B., J.C.D., The Interdict, V-163 pp., 1930.

57. O'Neil, Rev. William H., J.C.D., Papal Rescripts of Favor, VII-218 pp., 1930.

58. Bastnagel, Rev. Clement Vincent, J.U.D., The Appointment of Parochial Adjutants and Assistants, XV-257 pp., 1930.

59. Ferry, Rev. William A., A.B., J.C.D., Stole Fees, V-135 pp., 1930.

60. Costello, Rev. John Michael, A.B., J.C.D., Domicile and Quasi-Domicile, VII-201 pp., 1930.

61. Kremer, Rev. Michael Nicholas, A.B., S.T.B., J.C.D., Church Support in the United States, VI-1930.

62. Angulo, Rev. Luis, C.M., J.C.D., Legislacion de la Iglesia sobre la intencion en la aplication de la Santa Misa, VII-104 pp., 1931.

63. Frey, Rev. Wolfgang Norbert, O.S.B., A.B., J.C.D., The Act of Religious Profession, VIII-174 pp., 1931.

64. Roberts, Rev. James Brendan, A.B., J.C.D., The Banns of Marriage, XIV-140 pp., 1931.

65. Ryder, Rev. Raymond Aloysius, A.B., J.C.D., Simony, IX-151 pp., 1931.

66. Campagna, Rev. Angelo, Ph.D., J.U.D., Il Vicario Generale del Vescovo, VII-205 pp., 1931.

67. Cox, Rev. Joseph Godfrey, A.B., J.C.D., The Administration of Seminaries, VI-124 pp., 1931.

68. Gregory, Rev. Donald J., J.U.D., The Pauline Privilege, XV-165 pp., 1931.

69. Donohue, Rev. John F., J.C.D., The Impediment of Crime, VII-110 pp., 1931.

70. Dooley, Rev. Eugene A., O.M.I., J.C.D., Church Law on Sacred Relics, IX-143 pp., 1931.

71. Orth, Rev. Raymond Clement, O.M.C., J.C.D., The Approbation of Religious Institutes, 171 pp., 1931.

72. Pernicone, Rev. Joseph M., A.B., J.C.D., The Ecclesiastical Prohibition of Books, XII-267 pp., 1932.

73. Clinton, Rev. Connell, A.B., J.C.D., the Paschal Precept, IX-108 pp., 1932.

74. Donnelly, Rev. Francis B., A.M., S.T.L., J.C.D., The Diocesan Synod, VIII-125 pp., 1932.

75. Torrente, Rev. Camilo, C.M.F., J.C.D., Las Processiones Sagradas, V-145 pp. 1932.

76. Murphy, Rev. Edwin J., C.PP.S., J.C.D., Suspension Ex Informata Conscientia, XI-122 pp., 1932.

77. Mackenzie, Rev. Eric F., A.M., S.T.L., J.C.D., The Delict of Heresy in its Commission, Penalization, Absolution, VII-124 pp., 1932.

78. Lyons, Rev. Avitus E., S.T.B., The Collegiate Tribunal of First Instance, XI-147 pp., 1932.

79. Connolly, Rev. Thomas A., J.C.D., Appeals, XI-195 pp., 1932.

80. Sangmeister, Rev. Joseph V., A.B., J.C.D, Force and Fear as Precluding Matrimonial Consent, V-211 pp., 1932.

81. Jaeger, Rev. Leo A., A.B., J.C.D., The Administration of Vacant and Quasi-Vacant Episcopal Sees in the United States, IX-229 pp., 1932.

82. Rimlinger, Rev. Herbert T., J.C.D., Error Invalidating Matrimonial Consent, VII-79 pp., 1932.

83. Barrett, Rev. John D. M., SS., J.C.D., A Comparative Study of the Third Plenary Council of Baltimore and the Code, IX-221 pp., 1932.

84. Carberry, Rev. John J., Ph.D., S.T.D., J.C.D., The Juridical Form of Marriage, X-177 pp., 1934.

85. Dolan, Rev. John L., A.B., J.C.D., The Defensor Vinculi, XII-157 pp., 1934.

86. Hannan, Rev. Jerome D., A.M., S.T.D., LL.B., J.C.D., The Canon Law of Wills, IX-517 pp., 1934.

87. Lemieux, Rev. Delisle A., A.M., J.C.D., The Sentence in Ecclesiastical Procedure, IX-131 pp., 1934.

88. O'Rourke, Rev. James J., A.B., J.C.D., Parish Registers, VII-109 pp., 1934.

89. Timlin, Rev. Bartholomew, O.F.M., A.M., J.C.D., Conditional Matrimonial Consent, X-381 pp., 1934.

90. Wahl, Rev. Francis X., A.B., J.C.D., The Matrimonial Impediments of Consanguinity and Affinity, VI-125 pp., 1934.

91. White, Rev. Robert J., A.B., LL.B., S.T.D., J.C.D., Canonical Ante-Nuptial Promises and the Civil Law, VI-152 pp., 1934.

92. Herrera, Rev. Antonio Parra, O.C.D., J.C.D., Legislacion Ecclesiastica sobre el Ayuno y la Abstinencia, XI-191 pp., 1935.

93. Kennedy, Rev. Edwin J., J.C.D., The Special Matrimonial Process in Cases of Evident Nullity, X-165 pp., 1935.

94. Manning, Rev. John J., A.B., J.C.D., Presumption of Law in Matrimonial Procedure, XI-111 pp., 1935.

95. Moeder, Rev. John M., J.C.D., The Proper Bishop for Ordination and Dismissorial Letters, VII-135 pp., 1935.

96. O'Mara, Rev. William A., A.B., J.C.D., Canonical Causes for Matrimonial Dispensations, IX-155 pp., 1935.

97. Reilly, Rev. Peter, J.C.D., Residence of Pastors, IX-81 pp., 1935.

98. Smith, Rev. Mariner T., O.P., S.T.L., J.C.D., The Penal Law for Religious, VII-169 pp., 1935.

99. Whalen, Rev. Donald W., A.M., J.C.D., The Value of Testimonial Evidence in Matrimonial Procedure, XIII-297 pp., 1935.
100. Cleary, Rev. Joseph F., J.C.D., Canonical Limitations on the Alienation of Church Property, VIII-141 pp., 1936.
101. Glynn, Rev. John C., J.C.D., The Promoter of Justice, XX-337 pp., 1936.
102. Brennan, Rev. James H., S.S., A.M., S.T.B., J.C.D., The Simple Convalidation of Marriage, VI-135 pp., 1937.
103. Brunini, Rev. Joseph Bernard, J.C.D., The Clerical Obligations of Canons 139 and 142, X-121 pp., 1937.
104. Connor, Rev. Maurice, A.B., J.C.D., The Administrative Removal of Pastors, VIII-159 pp., 1937.
105. Guilfoyle, Rev. Merlin Joseph, J.C.D., Custom, XI-144 pp., 1937.
106. Hughes, Rev. James Austin, A.B., A.M., J.C.D., Witnesses in Criminal Trials of Clerics, IX-140 pp., 1937.
107. Jansen, Rev. Raymond J., A.B., S.T.L., J.C.D., Canonical Provisions for Catechetical Instruction, VII-153 pp., 1937.
108. Kealy, Rev. John James, A.B., J.C.D., The Introductory Libellus in Church Court Procedure, XI-121 pp., 1937.
109. McManus, Rev. James Edward, C.SS.R., J.C.D., The Administration of Temporal Goods in Religious Institutes, XVI-196 pp., 1937.
110. Moriarity, Rev. Eugene James, J.C.D., Oaths in Ecclesiastical Courts, X-115 pp., 1937.
111. Rainer, Rev. Eligius George, C.SS.R., J.C.D., Suspension of Clerics, XVII-249 pp., 1937.
112. Reilly, Rev. Thomas F., C.SS.R., J.C.D., Visitation of Religious, VI-195 pp., 1938.
113. Moriarty, Rev. Francis E., C.SS.R., J.C.D., The Extraordinary Absolution from Censures, XV-334 pp., 1938.
114. Connolly, Rev. Nicholas P., J.C.D., The Canonical Erection of Parishes, X-132 pp., 1938.
115. Donovan, Rev. James Joseph, J.C.D., The Pastor's Obligation in Prenuptial Investigation, XII-322 pp., 1938.
116. Harrigan, Rev. Robert J., M.A., S.T.B., J.C.D., The Radical Sanation of Invalid Marriages, VIII-208 pp., 1938.
117 Boffa, Rev. Conrad Humbert, J.C.D., Canonical Provisions for Catholic Schools, X-211 pp., 1939.
118. Parsons, Rev. Anscar John, O.F.M. Cap., J.C.D., Canonical Elections, XII-236 pp., 1939.
119. Reilly, Rev. Edward Michael, A.B., J.C.D., The General Norms of Dispensation, X-156 pp., 1939.
120. Ryan, Rev. Gerald Aloysius, A.B., J.C.D., Principles of Episcopal Jurisdiction, XII-172 pp., 1939.
121. Burton, Rev. Francis James, C.S.C., A.B., J.C.D., A Commentary on Canon 1125, X-222 pp., 1940.
122. Miaskiewicz, Rev. Francis Sigismund, J.C.D., Supplied Jurisdiction According to Canon 209, XII-340 pp., 1940.
123. Rice, Rev. Patrick William, A.B., J.C.D., Proof of Death in Prenuptial Investigation, VIII-156 pp., 1940.

124. Anglin, Rev. Thomas Francis, M.S., J.C.D., The Eucharistic Fast, VIII-183 pp., 1941.
125. Coleman, Rev. John Jerome, J.C.D., The Minister of Confirmation, VI-153 pp., 1941.
126. Downs, Rev. John Emmanual, A.B., J.C.D., The Concept of Clerical Immunity, XI-163 pp., 1941.
127. Esswein, Rev. Anthony Albert, J.C.D., Extrajudicial Penal Powers of Ecclesiastical Superiors, X-144 pp., 1941.
128. Farrell, Rev. Benjamin Francis, M.A., S.T.L., J.C.D., The Rights and Duties of the Local Ordinary Regarding Congregations of Women Religious of Pontifical Approval, V-195 pp., 1941.
129. Feeney, Rev. Thomas John, A.B., S.T.L., J.C.D., Restitutio in Integrum, VI-169 pp., 1941.
130. Findlay, Rev. Stephen William, O.S.B., A.B., J.C.D., Canonical Norms Governing the Deposition and Degradation of Clerics, XVII-279 pp., 1941.
131. Goodwine, Rev. John, A.B., S.T.L., J.C.D., The Right of the Church to Acquire Property, VIII-119 pp., 1941.
132. Heston, Rev. Edwin Louis, C.S.C., Ph.D., S.T.D., J.C.D., The Alienation of Church Property in the United States, XII-222 pp., 1941.
133. Hogan, Rev. James John, A.B., S.T.L., J.C.D., Judicial Advocates and Procurators, VIII-200 pp., 1941.
134. Kealy, Rev. Thomas M., A.B., Litt.B., J.C.D., Dowry of Women Religious, IX-152 pp., 1941.
135. Keene, Rev. Michael James, O.S.B., J.C.D., Religious Ordinaries and Canon 198, V-164 pp., 1942.
136. Kerin, Rev. Charles A., S.S., M.A., S.T.B., J.C.D., The Privation of Christian Burial, XVI-279 pp., 1941.
137. Louis, Rev. William Francis, M.A., J.C.D., Diocesan Archives, X-101 pp. 1941.
138. McDevitt, Rev. Gilbert Joseph, A.B., J.C.D., Legitimacy and Legitimation, X-247 pp., 1941.
139. McDonough, Rev. Thomas Joseph, A.B., J.C.D., Apostolic Administrators, X-217 pp., 1941.
140. Meier, Rev. Carl Anthony, A.B., J.C.D., Penal Administrative Procedure Against Negligent Pastors, XI-240 pp., 1941.
141. Schmidt, Rev. John Rogg, A.B., J.C.D., The Principles of Authentic Interpretation in Canon 17 of the Code of Canon Law, XII-331 pp., 1941.
142. Slafkosky, Rev. Andrew Leonard, A.B., J.C.D., The Canonical Episcopal Visitation of the Diocese, X-197 pp., 1941.
143. Swoboda, Rev. Innocent Robert, O.F.M., J.C.D., Ignorance in Relation to the Imputability of Delicts, IX-271 pp., 1941.
144. Dube, Rev. Arthur Joseph, A.B., J.C.D., The General Principles for the Reckoning of Time in Canon Law, VIII-299 pp., 1941.
145. McBride, Rev. James T., A.B., J.C.D., Incardination and Excardination of Seculars, XX-585 pp., 1941.
146. Król, Rev. John J., J.C.L., The Defendant in Contentious Trials, IX-207 pp., 1942.

147. Comyns, Rev. Joseph J., C.SS.R., J.C.L., The Papal and Episcopal Administration of Church Property.
148. Barry, Rev. Garrett Francis, O.M.I., J.C.L., Violation of the Cloister.
149. Bolduc, Rev. Gaten, C.S.V., A.B., S.T.L., J.C.L., Les Etudes dans les religions clericales.
150. Boyle, Rev. David John, M.A., J.C.L., The Juridic Effects of Moral Certitude on Pre-Nuptial Guarantees.
151. Canavan, Rev. Walter Joseph, M.A., Litt.D., J.C.L., Profession of Faith.
152. Desrochers, Rev. Bruno, A.B., Ph.L., S.T.B., J.C.L., Le Premier Concile Plénier de Québec et le Code de Droit Canonique.
153. Dillon, Rev. Robert Edward, A.B., J.C.L., Common Law Marriage.
154. Dodwell, Rev. Edward John, Ph.D., S.T.B., J.C.L., The Time and Place for the Celebration of Marriage.
155. Donnellan, Rev. Thomas Andrew, A.B., J.C.L., The Obligation of the Missa pro Populo.
156. Eltz, Rev. Louis Anthony, A.B., J.C.L., Cooperators in Crimes According to Canon 2209.
157. Gass, Rev. Sylvester Francis, M.A., J.C.L., Ecclesiastical Pensions.
158. Guiniven, Rev. John Joseph, C.SS.R., J.C.L., The Precept of Hearing Mass on Sundays and Holy Days of Obligation.
159. Gulczynski, Rev. John Theophilus, J.C.L., The Desecration and Violation of Churches.
160. Hammill, Rev. John Leo, M.A., J.C.L., The Obligations of the Traveler according to Canon 14.
161. Haydt, Rev. John Joseph, A.B., J.C.L., Reserved Benefices.
162. Huser, Rev. Roger John, O.F.M., A.B., J.C.L., The Canonical Crime of Abortion.
163. Kearney, Rev. Francis Patrick, A.B., S.T.L., J.C.L., The Principles of Canon 1127.
164. Linahen, Rev. Leo James, S.T.L., J.C.L., De Absolutione Complicis In Peccato Turpi.
165. McCloskey, Rev. Joseph Aloysius, A.B., J.C.L., The Subject of Ecclesiastical Law according to Canon 12.
166. O'Neill, Rev. Francis Joseph, C.SS.R., J.C.L., The Dismissal of Religious in Temporary Vows.
167. Prince, Rev. John Edward, A.B., S.T.B., J.C.L., The Diocesan Chancellor.
168. Riesner, Rev. Albert Joseph, C.SS.R., J.C.L., Apostates and Fugitives from Religious Institutes.
169. Stenger, Rev. Joseph Bernard, J.C.L., The Mortgaging of Church Property.
170. Waldron, Rev. Joseph Francis, A.B., J.C.L., The Minister of Baptism.
171. Willett, Rev. Robert Albert, J.C.L., The Probative Value of Documents in Ecclesiastical Trials.
172. Woeber, Rev. Edward Martin, M.A., J.C.L., The Interpellations.

www.ingramcontent.com/pod-product-compliance
Lightning Source LLC
LaVergne TN
LVHW050219080826
844660LV00012B/436

* 9 7 8 0 8 1 3 2 2 3 4 0 7 *